Improve
LESS

Improve
LESS

The Focus and Align Framework™
for Sustainable Continuous Improvement

Chad Bareither

PORTAGE, MI

Published by Bareither Group Consulting
706 Barberry Avenue
Portage, Michigan 49002
bareithergroup.com
chad@bareithergroup.com
(269) 716-4014

Bareither Group Consulting books are available at special discounts for bulk purchase for sales promotions, premiums, fundraising, and educational needs. Special books or book excerpts also can be created to fit specific needs. For details and permission requests, write to the email address above.

Neither the publisher nor author is engaged in rendering professional advice or services to the individual reader. The ideas, procedures, and suggestions contained in this book should not be used as a substitute for the advice of competent legal counsel from an attorney admitted or authorized to practice in your jurisdiction. Neither the author nor the publisher shall be liable or responsible for any loss or damage allegedly arising from any information or suggestion in this book.

ISBN 979-8-9889998-0-5 (hardback)
ISBN 979-8-9889998-1-2 (paperback)
ISBN 979-8-9889998-2-9 (eBook)

Printed in the United States of America

—

Copyediting by James Gallagher
Cover design & illustrations by Ruben Ramos
Proofreading by Adeline Hull
Book design & publishing by Kory Kirby
SET IN UTOPIA STD

Thanks to my most supportive fan and most ardent critic,
my loving wife, Rachel,
without whose support,
challenge,
and encouragement,
I would not be where I am today.

With all things being equal,
the simplest explanation tends to be the right one.
—WILLIAM OF OCKHAM

Contents

Preface

I STARE DOWN AT *the text message on my phone with a light sigh.*

Me: Want to go for a walk at lunch?

My friend: Sorry. Can't

My friend: Too Busy

My friend: Back-to-back meetings all day, just got added to another subteam :(

This good friend of mine was hedged in at work. Between project delivery and team development and other initiatives, there was no time, least of all for continuous improvement. In meetings most of the day, they feel like they can't get anything done. Solid calendars mean they often have to do their "work" outside of the workday. When I finally do connect with my friend in person, she tells me how busy she has been and how she can't seem to catch up.

—

The story here is not unique, but this conversation has stuck with me. If you ask one of your friends or colleagues how they are doing, there is a high likelihood they will answer "busy." **Yuck!**

Busyness has become both a sort of humble brag and an existential reassurance.[1,2] We justify our importance or excuse our performance limitations based on the congestion of our calendar. I have always hated being too busy. First, it does not afford me the appropriate time to plan or reflect. Second, being busy does not necessarily correlate to being productive, as seen in the story above. We can fill our days and not walk away fulfilled. Yet while this busyness epidemic influences both our personal and professional worlds, there is opportunity to defuse it. In this book I speak on how you should not try to change or improve *everything*, because you will actually make more measurable progress when improving *fewer* things.

That is the entire premise of my approach. Continuous Improvement always feels like extra work. And that extra work is always the first to get dropped. I strive to help myself and other leaders get their time back and better results by *improving less*. Change fewer things but the *right* things.

This insight comes from a career as an internal change agent at several large organizations, including Fortune 500 companies. With the technical knowledge and applied experience I've earned, I find that most organizations try to do too much. They overestimate what they can manage and sustain, thus underdelivering on what they

---

1 Tim Kreider, "The 'Busy' Trap," *New York Times*, 2012.
2 Jessica Stillman, "Science Confirms It: Talking about How Busy You Are Is a Humble Brag," Inc.com, December 19, 2016.

can achieve. Instead, they should be aligning their organizations with the opportunities that will make progress toward a vision and use the remaining time (from not trying to change everything) to invest in sustaining the great improvements they attained.

Frankly, most of the problems in business can be solved with *simple* tools. Increasingly more complex tools are not what is needed. What is lacking is an underlying system to unify our efforts on the important things. Operational excellence and change management programs are often implemented as "bolt-on" solutions in hopes of changing the organization through osmosis. What is required is a restructuring of the actual business management system. Leaders need the time and processes to (1) think strategically, (2) improve their businesses, and (3) manage daily interruptions.

When I think about how these elements come together, it makes me think about . . . motorcycles. It makes me think back to riding through central Wisconsin in my parents' Dodge Caravan and hearing a Harley-Davidson on the highway for the first time, revving its throttle beneath an underpass, the exhaust echoing with a concussive rattle as it scales from a growl to a roar. There are few things that are more iconically American than a Harley-Davidson motorcycle.

Harley-Davidson was founded in 1903 and survived the Great Depression, thrived in World War II, and achieved substantial expansion in the 1950s and 1960s. Yet this brand almost came to an end in 1981 when the company was on the brink of bankruptcy. American Machine and Foundry purchased the company and went through years of bottom line cost-cutting to exploit the brand reputation and maximize profits. They also slashed the workforce, leading to a labor strike. Harley-Davidson was in dire financial straits, $90 million in debt, and more than half of the "hogs" that rolled off the assembly line failed quality inspection.[3] The writing was on the wall, and top leadership was determined to right the sinking ship.

> We had to improve the quality of our product to be fair to the customer. If we hadn't improved the reliability of Harley-Davidson products, the company wouldn't be here today.
> —Richard Teerlink, former CFO turned CEO[4]

To survive and return to glory, Harley-Davidson had to tighten up their operations. They had to align on *strategy*, they had to invest in *process*, they had to *manage* the business closer to the work. They began a strategic transformation. The goals were simple: Improve quality. Release new designs faster. As the leadership teams benchmarked competitors or leaders in other industries, they aligned their tactics. Reduction of in-process inventory would make them more responsive to customer orders and streamline time to market for new models.

All the excessive inventory was covering up deeper wounds in their process. Harley adopted and branded an approach known as Materials as Needed (MAN). This sought to lower inventory so they could address challenges with product flow, underperforming operations, and supplier quality, all of which allowed them to clear floor space, identify production bottlenecks, and reduce costs of storage and warehousing.[5]

Simultaneously they invested in people by boosting labor

3 Judith Aquino, "The 10 Most Successful Rebranding Campaigns Ever," https://www.businessinsider.com/, February 10, 2011.

4 James Hagerty, "Harley Goes Lean to Build Hogs," *Wall Street Journal*, September 21, 2012.

5 Daniel Gross, "The Turnaround at Harley-Davidson," *Forbes Greatest Business Stories of All Time* (New Jersey: Wiley, 1997).

relations and empowering the floor. Process changes were developed *with* the people involved and not implemented before they understood and approved the changes. To flatten the organization and get leadership closer to the work, they simplified their HR structure from sixty-two job classifications to five job classifications.[6]

With their processes and quality on track, they had to rebuild confidence in the product with their customers. Aggressive ride campaigns to prove the change in quality were instituted. Owner groups were created by the company to get direct customer feedback and better understand needs. Demand began to rise for a quality American product that could now be backed by their operations.

Harley-Davidson went public in 1987 at an initial public offering of $0.36 per share. With the commitment to a unified strategy and a method to improve and manage processes, Harley saw their sales and stock rise all the way to $73.77 in 2006. At this point they had also reduced inventory levels 75 percent and shrunk floor space requirements 25 percent![7]

This process stability and supply chain agility is what also allowed Harley to rebound from the real estate bubble burst and the "Great Recession" in 2007-2009, as Americans were trimming luxury from their budgets and a severe slump in motorcycle sales was impending. Keith Wandell became chief executive and focused their management system on pivoting their fleet to more price point models and managing costs.[8] They leveraged the core of MAN inventory and workforce empowerment to solve process problems to create capacity, not reduce headcount.[9]

---

6 James Hagerty, "Harley Goes Lean to Build Hogs," *Wall Street Journal*, September 21, 2012.

7 Daniel Gross, "The Turnaround at Harley-Davidson," *Forbes Greatest Business Stories of All Time* (New Jersey: Wiley, 1997).

8 James Hagerty, "Harley Goes Lean to Build Hogs," *Wall Street Journal*, September 21, 2012.

9 Josh Patrick, "Small Business Lessons from Harley-Davidson's Turnaround," *New York Times*, September 25, 2012.

With maturity in process development and process improvement, they accelerated their rate of new model introduction. The type of rapid product introduction and high-mix product lines would not have been possible with the capabilities Harley had in the 1980s. In today's operations they have the capability of releasing up to four new models per year.[10] Harley-Davidson continues to double-down on their operational process focus to enable their top-level strategies to strengthen its strongest sales segments, expand geographic footprint, and promote the lifestyle brand through parts and accessories, merchandise, and rider groups and experiences. This type of repeat ascension to greatness was possible through a system that created and deployed a unified *strategy*, a structured methodology to make *process improvements*, and a framework to *manage* performance. These are the key tenets of every successful business system.

The approach in this book is based on industry-leading continuous improvement methodologies. The practices and tools encompassed in the Industrial Engineering, Lean, and Six Sigma Body of Knowledge have been collected and refined over a century of practice and learning. Yet today Lean and Six Sigma programs have become "brands" for marketing and selling services and seminars. There is such a broad application found under these banners that it is a discredit to the industry and a disservice to our clients, causing more confusion and infighting.

I submit in this book, in this approach, a small departure, a simplified text intended to be read in a weekend so you can come back and start implementing on Monday. No Japanese translation, no advanced statistics, no corporate program with branded hats,

---

10 "Stripped-Down Harley Rebounds from Recession," Associated Press, June 10, 2013.

T-shirts, and mouse pads. Enclosed is an overview of an effective business management system, demonstrated by the success of clients across six industries. Leaders and change agents spend too much time and energy on improvements but insufficient time aligning and communicating strategy, then managing their daily performance. The sustainment of performance gains comes through alignment of effort and systems.

Your biggest barrier to continuous improvement will be *starting*. Nothing changes if you don't change something, and change takes time and effort. So read on, start small, then iterate. But don't let perfect be the enemy of good (or even of starting). Refining your application through experience is faster and more effective than long planning and a massive launch. Don't overvalue traditional learning over wisdom gained through application. This is an investment in your business and yourself. Everything you need to start comes next, so go get your time back.

No match was ever lit with "maybe."
—Arleigh Kincheloe

1

Business Management System

WALKING ACROSS THE POLISHED *concrete production floor, I look up as another associate stops my tour guide for a quick hello and an embrace. He loves his job and perhaps loves the people even more. It showed from the response he was receiving in his old stomping grounds. Today we were going to see the high-density storage (HDS) solution that he helped put in place at one of the global assembly plants. This solution reduced total inventory on hand, reduced lead time for replenishment to assembly lines, enabled high schedule attainment, and utilized significantly less floor space.*

We clear the last cordial interruption to meet with the HDS team lead. Before we even get into talks about process and performance, we receive bad news. It's conveyed through a defeated expression that the decision was made to move inventory back to an off-site warehouse; HDS will cease operations.

My guide's face drops to match his colleague's, enthusiasm replaced with confusion. New management had taken over. They disagreed with the approach and replaced a system that had taken years to develop and hone with a more traditional operating model to mitigate delivery risk with more inventory, build up on-hand inventory, and move it to an off-site warehouse for replenishment.

It wasn't that the process management had failed. There were hiccups, but the same would be the case for a third-party logistics operation. It wasn't that the improvement wasn't realized. On average, replenishment lead times were down and schedule attainment was up. It wasn't that the strategy wasn't aligned. There was an absence of consistency in operating systems between the plants to make these decisions. This created a scenario for a flip-flop in strategy that wouldn't end with this current iteration of best practice.

—

Your first thought on a Monday morning might not be "How is my business *running*?" It is more likely a version of "How is my business *doing*?" Measures like sales, profit, quality, on-time deliveries, safety. These are all the *results* of your business processes, but they are not how your business operates. They are not the system you use to manage your business.

In the rush to launch your company or fulfill orders or scale up or even cut back, you, as a leader, often get pulled into daily decision-making to get those results. This is an opportunity to step back from the current crises in your business to ask *how* decisions get made daily, not just *what* decisions need to be made right now. For you to scale or be more agile in execution or just get time back in your day, you need a business management system.

A system is a set of independent elements working together in a larger mechanism. These may be physical pieces or parts in a machine, political beliefs and laws in a governmental structure, or principles and processes in a business. In any system there is an overarching design for delivering or maintaining something of value—products for consumers, services for customers, quality of life for clients.

You have a system for *how* you run your business. It may be precisely tuned and operating predictably. Or it may be haphazardly cobbled together, requiring manual intervention to maintain daily operations. More often than not, organizations (maybe even yours) have an ad hoc system for their business management. This can lead to delays at the front line while "decision makers" and top leadership spend so much time "in the weeds" that they lose capacity for longer-term thinking.[11]

You put a process in place as a response to a mistake or accident. You write a policy to address an issue that crept up. You hold an annual retreat once a year to align priorities. All reactions to a problem that has already burned you. This reactive approach to system development is like driving down the road looking only in the rearview mirror. You can drive only so fast or so far before you veer off course or have a collision.

A neighbor of mine is a real estate agent. Most of his business is

---

11 Martin Reeves, Simon Levin, Thomas Fink, and Ania Levina, "Taming Complexity," *Harvard Business Review*, January–February 2020.

from long-term relationships. That means that many of his clients are older or the children of previous clients. His services are often needed when they are moving out of their family homes and downsizing into something more manageable. He tells me that by the time most people choose to take action, they are one to five years "too late." The mental and physical stress may be too high at that point, and often the property has experienced disrepair or excess clutter. They should have started the process sooner.

Likewise, putting a business system in place is something you should be thinking about before you need it. Before the crisis, before you hit a constraint on growth, before you start to scale. If you are struggling to manage the day-to-day or can't get leadership aligned on a strategic direction or are taking shotgun approaches to improving processes and products, it is time to step back from working *in your business* and invest time working *on your business*. Having a system in place to run the business creates a structure for responsibility and decision-making. It makes operating the business more predictable for the leadership and for the employees. This structure of a business management system consists of three elements: (1) a method to develop and deploy strategy, (2) a method for making improvement to processes and products, and (3) a method to manage daily execution for consistent performance.

Strategy Deployment

This aligns the organization with a common purpose through defining mission, vision, and values. With that shared vision, the important work is prioritized to realize the next milestone in pursuit of a future-state performance. The team gets in sync by evaluating your strengths, weaknesses, opportunities, and threats, then deploying a set of cascading objectives, goals, strategies, and measures. We dig in further and practice this in chapter two.

Process Improvement

This is a method that uses structure and discipline to clarify the specific problems you are trying to resolve and break them down to the root cause. The methodology is referred to by the acronym DMAIC, which stands for define, measure, analyze, improve, and control. There are specific objectives to accomplish and questions to answer in each phase. This keeps the improvement team focused and stakeholders aligned as you move forward. The approach is scalable and repeatable for a variety of problem types and complexities. This element is detailed out in chapter three.

Daily Management

This entails the processes that control your daily business performance. We seek to understand why you get the results you do, to control the crucial processes, and to monitor those tasks or activities closely. Transparency of performance through visualization and a regular schedule of reporting are used to help identify, then resolve or escalate, issues before they affect results. In turn, teams are engaged to understand the process and are empowered to make decisions, a responsibility not strictly reserved for management or senior leadership. More on the process management element can be found in chapter four.

—

Figure 1.1 illustrates the structure of the business management system and the three included elements. The vertical axis represents the level of responsibility in the organization, moving from frontline staff up to senior leadership. Depending on your organization this may be three to five layers of management (four layers are shown here for illustration). Moving horizontally across any of those layers you see the percentage of time that should be spent in that element. For example, frontline staff should spend the majority of their time executing processes and utilizing daily management tools, then spend some time engaged in improvement of those processes. There is a small fraction of strategy deployment to ensure it is communicated and understood. Senior leadership should spend most of their time developing and deploying strategy, then some time involved in key process improvement initiatives and projects. Minimal time should be devoted to management of the business processes and daily decision-making.

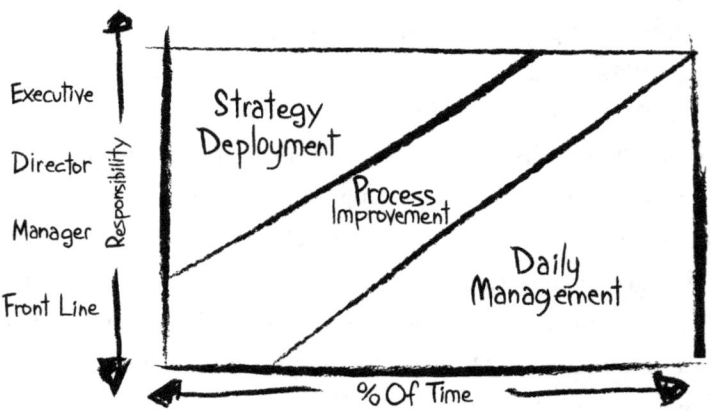

Figure 1.1: Business Management System Framework

These three elements are all required, and they work together as a system. This system organizes simple tools to enable deployment and sustainment of business processes and establish standard roles and responsibilities in decision-making. The percentages for time allocation are not fixed in the model because this is a guideline for you and your team to reflect and learn about where they are investing their time.

When senior leadership gets drawn into daily management of the processes, it eats away at their bandwidth for strategy deployment. This can lead to management burnout or a culture of firefighting. When frontline staff are too wrapped up in strategy deployment, we lose capacity for management of daily activity and continuous improvement of our processes. Yet we also see that the elements are not distinct horizontal responsibilities.

Directors and managers need to be involved in strategy deployment to provide critical feedback and gain understanding of why certain things are prioritized. Managers and directors need to engage in daily management to coach their teams and understand barriers or challenges so they can allocate resources appropriately to resolve issues. Process improvement is what connects strategy to management. Improvements are defined both top-down where a gap exists between target and actual performance of a goal, and bottom-up as operational problems surface within our processes.

Overall, you see that the smallest portion of business management is process improvement. More thought and effort needs to be paid to identifying the "right" opportunities through strategy and sustaining changes with daily management. Clearly defining and articulating strategy narrows the focus of where to invest for improvements. Regularly managing your processes ensures sustainment of those improvements and escalates new issues for resolution. As indicated by the title for this book, Improve LESS!

Misalignment between the guidelines for time allocation and actual management behavior presents an opportunity for change and improvement. Do this for me. Hold yourself accountable here as leaders and be open to learning where your time is spent. Use the Leader Time Reflection Worksheet (see Figure 1.2) as a starting point to understand where you invest your time on a regular basis. This is a great step to increase your awareness and highlight the biggest opportunity to reallocate or get some of your time back.

Reflecting on your calendar and actual behavior throughout the week will provide a directionally accurate representation of your priorities. This will help take volatility out of your schedule and performance. Go ahead and try it. It is best to reflect at the end of the week and use that information to plan or set aside time in advance for the following week before your inbox is overcome with urgent issues.

Over time each organizational layer can identify recurring issues that prevent them from having predictable weeks and work to resolve or delegate those challenges. That is why we ask two questions: (1) How much time did you spend on this category? (2) What were some of the repeatable tasks performed? You will identify issues that should have been resolved elsewhere in the business, so delegate. You may also identify issues that need to be resolved and prevent them from occurring and disrupting your schedule.

	Strategy	Improvement	Management	Notes/Action
	What were some of the repeatable tasks performed? How much time did you spend on this category?			
Week of _____				
Week of _____				
Week of _____				

Figure 1.2: Leader Time Reflection Worksheet

The remainder of this book will include an overview of each of the individual elements, the frameworks to employ these elements, a simple set of recommended tools and templates, and who is accountable to lead and participate. After an overview of these elements we show how they integrate together. This is done through a five-step process known as the Focus and Align Framework™. That is how we deploy the system and begin leading the business with confidence . . . and, eventually, less of your time.

The hard part is always sustainment. In the closing chapter we discuss the change required in leadership behavior that enables this system to sustain and thrive. The culture and behaviors that you set out to intentionally create must be reflected in your own actions. In addition to your unique organizational values, underpinning mindsets are fundamental to change and sustainment. We demonstrate how to exercise these to build your company muscle for continuous improvement. This includes the concept of Leader Standard Work to help you develop the habits of sustaining improvement through process confirmation and daily management reviews.

> We build our systems the way we build our cities: over time,
> without a plan, on top of ruins.
> —Ellen Ullman

2 Strategy Deployment

FLOATING ALONG ON A *pontoon boat at sunset, board members of a local organization are catching up and celebrating successes of the past year. The sun drifts lazily toward the horizon on the long Michigan summer night, and ice clinks against the sides of glasses. The conversation between the current CEO and board members has turned to the future.*

Challenges in initiating new programs were holding the organization back from delivery of better results and stronger financial performance. They could source new contracts, but mobilization of the internal team always felt like playing catch-up, with some false starts on their record.

Some board members who had backgrounds in manufacturing spoke about the methods and transformations in their work environments. One of the board members discussed an approach that entailed process management and continuous improvement. The concept of Lean management was introduced.

Two weeks later I am talking with the CEO and all the program directors. My colleague and I were "loaned" to this organization to explore process management and improvement through Lean management methods. We began by digging into the struggle with new program introduction. After letting some of the dust settle from venting frustrations, the process was mapped to understand the flow and functional handoffs. We found pain points, identified gaps between current capabilities and expected results, scoped out improvement efforts that were required, and agreed on an approach for regular, visual review with the team.

It was clear when the "project" was completed that the "work" was just beginning. We had uncovered the challenges in the program development process, but a more significant revelation was when the entire leadership team began to understand why it was so important to bring programs in on a faster timeline. Everyone was working to do the best in their lane, yet there was a lack of alignment at a strategic level.

We spun off of that initial engagement and immediately went to work on strategy deployment. We confirmed the mission, values, and vision for the organization, then defined the critical objectives for the next three years, and created annual goal targets. The leadership team scoped the projects and initiatives to achieve those goals and defined how to measure their execution.

We posted the plan and milestones on a prominent wall in the main office, with scheduled review meetings to provide updates and escalate issues for help. At the presentation for the board of directors three months later, we shared the process, the lessons along the way, the elements of the strategic plan, and how we were going to manage it to keep everyone informed and accountable. There was unanimous endorsement from the board, and a huge amount of pride and understanding from the staff. They were aligned. They were focused.

—

Where do you want to be in five years?

I remember a point in my career when that cliché interview question would frustrate me. I also remember the time when it changed and became more profound for me. Visualizing and articulating a future state is psychologically proven to aid in achieving it.[12] As I began mentoring others, it was pivotal to understand where they wanted to go so they could be more intentional about the experience they gathered and the opportunities they pursued.

Intentional. That was it. That was the word for having clarity on your professional journey. As a leader in any size company or team, it is even more important to have clarity on where your organization is going so you can effectively communicate your direction. Then you can all move with intention, collectively.

A strategy is a plan of action or policy designed to pursue a desired end state. Strategy is something organizations in every industry talk about. In fact, a lot of organizations, probably even yours, have a strategy or strategic plan. Yet only about 10 percent of organizations achieve the majority of their strategic objectives.[13,14]

---

12 Shakti Gawain, *Creative Visualization: Use the Power of Your Imagination to Create What You Want in Your Life* (San Francisco: New World Library, 2016).

13 https://boardview.io/blog/strategy-execution-stats/, accessed July 18, 2022.

14 https://www.gartner.com/smarterwithgartner/the-five-pillars-of-strategy-execution, accessed July 18, 2022.

But why? If strategy is literally our prioritized goals and initiatives, how can it be that a slim fraction of companies are even achieving their goals and remain in business?

Benchmarking shows that many of the same companies that are achieving their objectives and goals are also the ones leading their industry or segment. Is it random chance that an organization hits their goals, that they can repeatedly hit their goals, and that they also lead their peers? Are those organizations just lucky? Or is there something different in their plan?

Failing to achieve your strategic goals can be caused by faulty assumptions, insufficient communication, or weak execution. To address many of these failure modes, we need to think about strategic deployment, not just strategic planning. Deployment brings communication and accountability into the approach itself. This ensures alignment vertically, through chain of command, and horizontally, between functions across the organization. The approach also establishes communication channels for adjustments to targets or plans and escalation of issues.

Figure 2.1: Strategy Deployment

The process for strategy deployment follows a five-phase cycle. This process begins with establishing an organizational vision. That is the compass heading and long-term destination the organization is pursuing. With a vision clarified, we develop objectives. These are things we want to accomplish, and they will confirm we are on track for the destination of our vision.

Third, annual goals are developed to quantitatively confirm that we have achieved an objective. Some objectives may require more than one planning year to accomplish, in which case the goal is how much and how far we will go this year.

Note the "feedback loop" of objectives and goals. The targets are a discussion between the layers of the organization developing them. Senior leadership tends to take a higher-elevation perspective of where we want to go, while management is closer to the work and understands current capabilities and realistic stretch targets. This discussion and learning cycle eventually converge on annual goals that are aspirational but also realistic. While objectives are qualitative targets to accomplish or become, goals are quantitative measures of those objectives. Projects or initiatives are how we intend to achieve a goal, and they're referred to as strategies.

The next layer of the organization gets involved to implement programs, projects, or initiatives that will help achieve each goal. Each strategy should have at least one measure that indicates whether the work is on track or off track. Implementing these strategies and measures means that plans should be developed and ownership/accountability defined at the appropriate level of the organization.

The cycle of Plan-Do-Check-Act (PDCA) repeats throughout the planning horizon. The teams iteratively check progress and effectiveness of strategies to learn what is working and to escalate concerns that may prevent them from achieving a goal. Finally, we look back at the previous planning cycle (typically a one-year cadence) of our objectives, goals, strategies, and measures to inform decisions made for the next cycle. The key pieces of information provided for the team through a deployed strategy are (1) where we are going and (2) how we intend to get there.

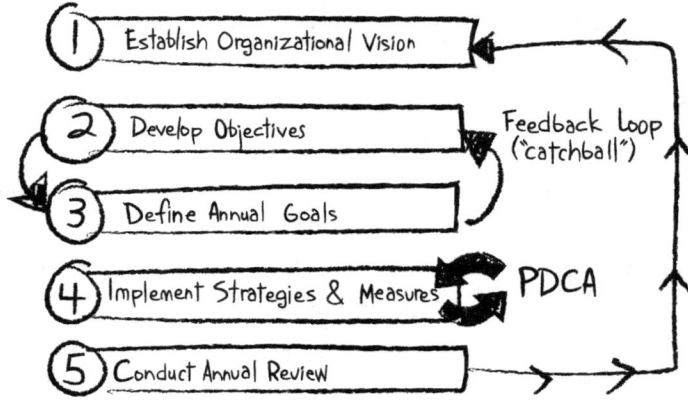

Figure 2.2: Strategy Deployment Cycle

"Where are we going?"

"Why?"

"How long will it take to get there?"

"Are we there yet?"

I can hear these questions echo in my head from family road trips or outings. After we've climbed into our family car, the questions begin firing from those smaller passengers in the back seat. As the leader of the family, or the leader of the organization, you are obliged to have some sort of answer to these questions. Strategy deployment assists with just that.

Where you are going is established by your vision and objectives. Why you are pursuing that destination is answered by your mission and values. How you intend to get there and how long it will take are reflected in your strategies and measures. If we back up to the start of the approach, we can see all these components and how they combine to form the strategy deployment element.

Mission, Vision, Values

These three components create a common lens through which your team should view the world. Mission declares the organization's particular role in the world, its purpose. It creates a North Star for commitment to customers and employees. A first deterrent to getting distracted or off track in your strategy is to ensure the organization knows their core focus.

Developing your mission requires you to think about why your company exists for its customers or the cause you serve. A mission statement is a concise version of who you serve and what you do for them. The vision stems from the anchor point of your mission statement and looks to what you want to accomplish. We execute the mission today—and every day. If you stay on mission and improve performance, what does your customer or cause look like in the future? That aspirational future is your vision.

You can align your team around these statements of purpose and destination. Values, then, are how the teams interact with customers, coworkers, and their communities. These are a set of guiding principles that shape the work environment and create the repeated behaviors that establish culture. Defining values are important to pressure test your strategies later. Is "how" we are getting there aligned with what we say is important?

If you have never done work as a leadership team to establish mission, vision, and values, this will not be a superficial task. Creating this lens of priorities for the company helps you and your team understand what to say "yes" to and, more importantly, what to say "no" to. I may need to say that again. Strategy is, more importantly, what we are saying "no" to. So devote time to collectively run through the worksheet in Figure 2.3 in that order: mission, vision, values. The bulleted questions guide the conversation. Each participant documents their input in the blank sections, then shares and combines for a collective result.

Mission	Vision
What is the purpose of your organization? What customer/client/cause do you serve? When is a time your company was at it's best?	What are you doing that no one in this space is doing? What is the end-state of your mission? When are you done? What will your customers/your cause look like in the future?

Circle words that describe who you serve from each entry
Underline words what you do or solve

Using input from above, write a statement:
Include who/what you serve and what you help solve/achieve

Values	
How does your team show up everyday? What makes your team and how they interact unique?	What tangible behaviors can you see? How will you demonstrate this value to others?
1)	
2)	
3)	
4)	
5)	

Figure 2.3: Mission, Vision, Values Worksheet

Objectives

A vision is an aspirational future state of the organization or the world it serves. The achievement of that vision can be confirmed through milestones known as objectives. These are impartial outcomes that the entire organization can point to and say whether they have demonstrated or delivered.

To get from mission and vision to objectives, a wonderful exercise is the SWOT analysis. SWOT stands for strengths, weaknesses, opportunities, and threats. Strengths are internal capabilities beneficial to your mission and vision. Weaknesses are internal conditions harmful to your pursuit of mission and vision. Opportunities are external influences that are potentially helpful for you. Threats are external influences that are potentially harmful.

Outlining the SWOT for your business as a team further clarifies the lens that you are looking at your industry and mission field through. You may choose to leverage strengths, improve a weakness, take advantage of opportunities, or mitigate potential threats. What you want to do is phrased as an objective, which is commonly a qualitative statement of something to accomplish. That could be an absolute statement on growth or improvement over current state or achievement of a rating/ranking. It could also be a relative statement as a comparison against peers or benchmark or historical performance.

Objectives confirm that the organization is en route to the vision. Objectives further narrow the focus of your team. It is good to know where you are heading. It is even better to clearly state how far you are going this year. While an individual objective may take several years to achieve, those milestones can be broken down into annual targets we call goals.

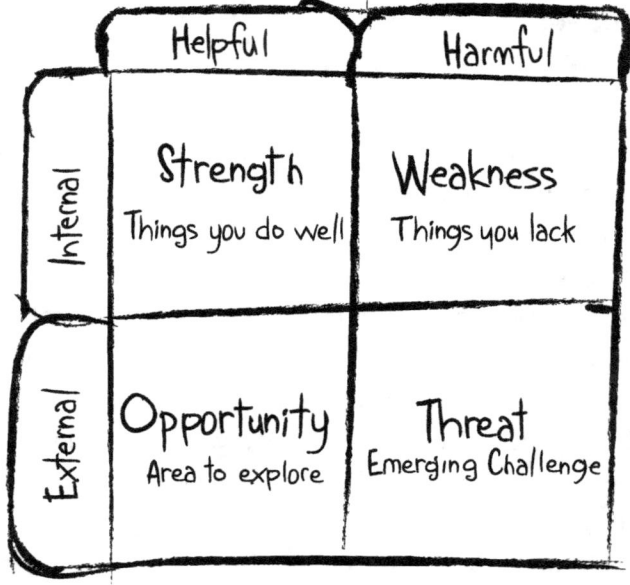

Figure 2.4: SWOT Analysis Definitions

Goals

A goal is something you intend to accomplish within the planning cycle, typically one year. Goals are numbers that define what success looks like, and they usually entail financial or operational metrics. An effective way to visualize goals, and the subsequent strategies and measures, is a key performance indicator (KPI) tree. A KPI tree is a visual map that shows the relationship between requirements that influence a goal, the processes that support/ deliver those requirements, and the control or confirmation evidence you can observe on that process (see Figure 2.5). It is not necessary to measure and improve all the elements, processes, and evidence to achieve a goal. Strategically, we focus on the portions of the tree with the biggest opportunity to influence the goal or biggest opportunity to close a gap in performance (to achieve a benchmark or return to a desired condition).

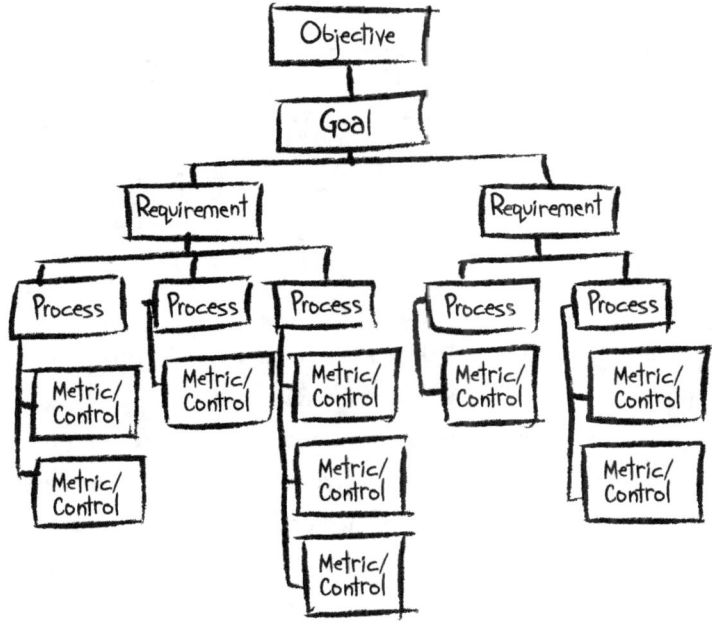

Figure 2.5: KPI Tree Format

An example is provided in Figure 2.6 for safety, measured through the lagging indicator of recordable incidents. It is intuitive that simply measuring adverse events that already happened is a poor way to control safety. Deconstructing your safety system into requirements, processes, and evidence helps to identify gaps where control does not exist or performance is not where you desire. Circles are placed to identify the portions of the tree that would be strategically tackled at a process level to influence the goal.

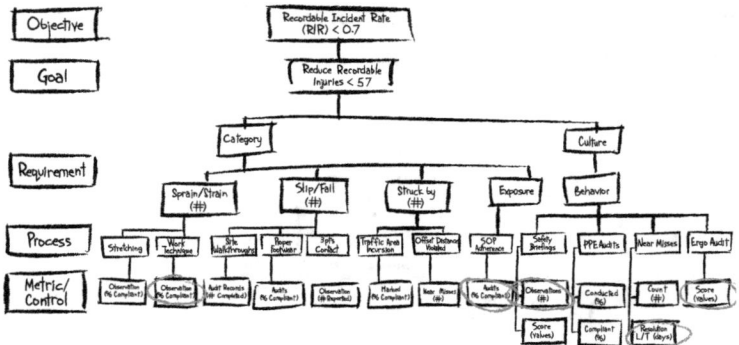

Figure 2.6: KPI Tree Example, Safety

It should also be reinforced here that the feedback loop is important. Objectives are aligned with the entire team at that level of leadership. Goals are developed and KPI trees built with input from the team. Challenges occur both ways, with leadership stretching goals for a bigger advancement and the supporting team pulling them in to make them achievable. The intent is to arrive at a target that is inspirational but realistic.

Strategies & Measures

To achieve different results, the underlying work processes need to change. With goals established, the leadership team engages with their next level to outline *how* they can achieve those goals. Strategies are projects or initiatives or programs that are put into place to change the way the organization works, resulting in different outcomes. Depending on the organization, strategies may be organized and chartered to provide authority for resources and work plans. These strategic choices on *how* to deliver the goals also define measures to monitor progress. Measures indicate if the progress of a strategy is on track and move the organization toward achieving a goal.

Looking back to Figure 2.6, the circles identify points of the KPI tree that will be targeted with a strategy to change the associated measure. The leadership team can then see how they expect effort at those points to affect process performance requirement deliverables and, ultimately, the goal. The clarity of this thread of impact is valuable for communicating to the team why we are focusing on certain strategies and not others.

PDCA Cycle

After defining strategies and measures, your organization will have a cohesive plan to pursue a shared vision. It is marked by objective milestones of success and annual goals to indicate whether you are on track. Strategies and measures move at a higher cadence and require more routine evaluation and management.

The PDCA Cycle, also known as the Deming Cycle,[15] is a repeating process to evaluate and correct the effectiveness of our work. We *plan* what work will be done and what results we expect. Then we *do* the work according to the plan and applicable standards. The most important step is to *check* our results.

On a strategic level the cadence of review for measures and goals is monthly, even weekly if the work processes allow. That is, if the performance data changes monthly, review monthly; if it changes weekly, review weekly; if it changes daily, review daily.

Now that we have checked to see if our results met our plan, we can *act*. We change the inputs, resources, or the process to get a different result, update the *plan*, and repeat for the next cycle. This

---

15 The Man: Articles: "The Three Careers of W. Edwards Deming," W. Edwards Deming Institute, accessed October 15, 2008.

cyclic learning aligns the organization to understand capabilities and performance, which enables improvement. That clarifies where you as a leader should spend your time. Structure your days and weeks to check in on the important strategies, and you won't be surprised by the results at quarter or year end.

Annual Review

Strategy deployment is usually an annual process. Most organizations review annual performance for fiscal year decisions or to report to stakeholders. This reflection is internal looking and evaluates progress toward strategy and vision. This review and learning aligns the team on what is working, what is not working, and where more resources need to be applied to achieve goals and objectives for the following cycle. The process, the tools, and the targets are meant to evolve as you as an individual leader and your organization progress with this process.

—

To manage and document your application of strategy deployment, use the OGSM Worksheet template shown in Figure 2.7. Your mission and vision are placed at the top of the sheet. They are your true north, and all content below should relate back to enabling those two statements. Your set of objectives that represent the vision defined with your leadership team are placed in the left-hand column. These are qualitatively what you want to accomplish on the next step toward your vision. For each objective, establish that at least one goal is defined for that planning cycle/year.

Goals are entered into the second column. These define quantitatively what you want to accomplish. Where multiple goals relate to a given objective, the column cell is split horizontally to show that they both measure the pursuit/accomplishment of the same objective. As a rule of thumb you should keep objectives to five or fewer. Similarly, there should not be more than three goals for an individual objective. The complexity that comes with too many goals erodes the focus of leadership and your teams. Start simple and scale to what you can manage effectively . . . remember: improve LESS. The objectives and goals of the first two columns represent *what* you want to accomplish for the strategy timeline (often one year).

Now take time to reflect on the objectives and goals and have the leadership team socialize them with their next level in the organization. Once aligned on goal definition and targets, work to identify key strategies (projects, initiatives, programs) to get there, and establish measures of success and ownership for those projects. Similarly, there may be a many-to-one relationship between strategies and goals. Likewise, a strategy may support two goals within an objective.

To identify what strategies to focus on, use a KPI tree as a way to visualize the entire landscape of processes that affect your goals. Building a KPI tree for each goal gets the leadership team aligned on what affects a given performance measure and where they believe they should focus.

Aligning cross-functionally on where you will apply resources in the KPI tree to effect the biggest change is a strategy. It clarifies both where you are going to invest and, equally, what you are not going to do. This is, in my experience, the hardest part of strategy deployment: to tailor it down. There are countless things we could do. Gaining consensus on where you will prioritize and focus resources for a collective improvement puts the leadership team in a team mentality. A hypothetical example is shown in Figure 2.8 to illustrate use of the tool.

Mission	
Vision	

Objective	Goal	Strategy	Measure	Owner

Figure 2.7: OGSM Worksheet

Objective	Goal	Strategy	Measure	Owner
Improve Cash Flow by $20M Invest in R&D	10% Cost Reduction in Supply Chain	Reduce Days on Hand Inventory	Days on Hand (DOH, days) Inventory Holling Cost ($)	VP Procurement
		Fleet Optimization	Vehicle Utilization (%) Monthly Lease Costs ($)	DIR Distribution
Be the Safest Place to Work	0.7 RIR (<57 Recordable Injuries)	5S Distribution Centers	5S Audit Scores	DIR EHS
		Safety Training & Audits	Training Rates (%) Near Miss Reporting (count)	
Lead Industry in Customer Satisfaction	Reduce shipment errors <1%	Improve Order Intake Process	Intake Error Rate (count)	VP Sales
Be the most desirable employer in the region	Employee Retention >90%	Employee Engagement Plan	Action Items PTQ	DIR HR

Figure 2.8: OGSM Example

An overlying principle is making your strategy and performance visual. Harboring knowledge or information segregates the organization to haves and have-nots. Leaders need to make their goals and performance visual to be vulnerable about our performance and the learning that results. This demonstrates the same level of accountability we desire for our frontline value creators.

The tool used for visualization is less important than the capabilities it provides. Your solution should enable you to identify the status, trend, and what you're doing about it within ten seconds. (More tactical details on visual management can be found in chapter four.) Status should indicate on track or off track from plan. This can be done with color coding or symbols. Trend indicates the historical performance. Are we off track and getting worse? Off track and getting better? On track and heading the wrong way? What you are doing about it entails the countermeasures (or act portion of PDCA).

If a status or trend indicates being off track, this demonstrates who and what the leader should "go see" to understand what we are doing to adjust the plan. An example strategic performance board is shown in Figure 2.9. Red status items are off track from the plan. This could mean that the Goal is off track and the Strategies are not being executed (off track). This presents an opportunity to understand what the capability or resource constraint is on the team. It could mean that the Goal is off track and the Strategies are on track. This implies that the changes are not having the desired effect on the goal and that the team needs to regroup and change strategy. It may also mean the target for the Goal is wrong. If you have learned more about the process, market, and technology, you may want to adjust the target. The owner and leadership team should prioritize red items to learn more and then take action as needed to correct trends.

Figure 2.9: Example Strategic Performance Board

Through strategy deployment the organization learns what the priorities are and, over time, what areas need the focus of improvement. Strategies (initiatives, projects, programs) are implemented to improve performance and align to goals. Within the planning cycle other issues may arise that require improvement. That is why a common improvement methodology is important in your organization. This enables collaboration among functions and locations on a platform of similar language and tools. With clarity on where you are going, what you want to accomplish, and how you intend to deliver those results, your team needs a predictable method for improving the processes you prioritized.

ALICE:
Would you tell me, please, which way I ought to go from here?
THE CHESHIRE CAT:
That depends a good deal on where you want to get to.
ALICE:
I don't much care where.
THE CHESHIRE CAT:
Then it doesn't much matter which way you go.
—Lewis Carroll

3 Process Improvement

I STARED AT THE words jotted down hastily in my notebook, trying not to get misty-eyed myself. "This is the most anyone has ever cared about my job and our pain points," the technician shared through visible emotion.

Wow!

A tear-filled reflection after the week-long improvement event was more than I was prepared for. It was fun to facilitate a great project. It was great to get the results that would impact the business. This, however, was transformational. The technicians were working against several months' worth of backlog in technical updates. Together, we were able to identify a few immediate countermeasures and some longer-term fixes that would increase their throughput by 28 percent.

With the aid of a short-term contingent labor workforce, burndown of the backlog could be achieved by the end of the year and stabilized. But more powerful than the results was that the technician felt "seen," that the manager had a clearer understanding of the actual frustrations they were up against. The upstream colleagues understood how defects and omissions in their process were contributing to the issue and impacting the business. It was remarkable that once the teams agreed they all had a problem to solve, there was breakthrough-level improvement. It took a standard approach with simple tools to deliver these results with confidence.

—

Human beings are naturally curious. We have innate desires to explore and manipulate and order and create things.[16] This pool of human energy and insight is a tremendously valuable resource for any organization. But, as in harvesting any resource, it requires intention and focus. Organizations and teams are able to cultivate and gather this human potential by first aligning that energy on priority areas of focus and then using consistent methods of application to make the experience predictable and familiar. To leverage our human potential for problem-solving and process improvement, we first align the teams by clearly defining our problems. Second, we use proven and consistent methodologies

16 "Basic Human Tendencies," https://www.montessoriprintshop.com/human-tendencies.html#:~:text=They%20can%20imagine%20that%20which%20does%20not%20exist%2C,own%20personal%20growth%20and%20want%20to%20perfect%20themselves, accessed August 12, 2022.

to create repeatable results and common language. Let's begin with the concept of a problem.

What is a problem? A key aspect of improving is the need to agree on what a "problem" is and when you have one. At the most basic level a problem is any time the actual result does not match what you expect. If I expect to drive to Chicago in two and a half hours and it actually takes four hours . . . that is a problem. If I expect to send $1,200 per month in my personal budget and I actually spend $2,000 on my credit card . . . that is a problem. If I expect to have no safety incidents on my manufacturing line and there is actually an injury . . . that is a problem. If I expect to answer a customer call in ten minutes and they are actually on hold for twenty-five minutes . . . that is a problem. The actual result does not meet the expected result, so there is a gap, and that gap is a problem.

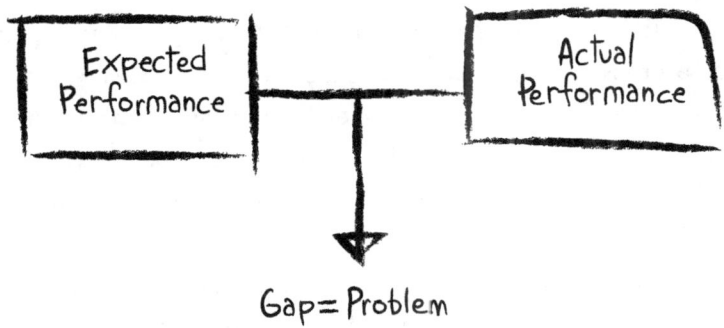

Figure 3.1: Problem Gap

That "gap" can be against a benchmark or historic performance target, implying that process performance has slipped or regressed to an undesirable state. You may also strategically create the gap by setting an improvement target (a new level of expected performance). Recall from the strategy deployment element in the previous chapter that this may be needed for some processes or evidence in our KPI tree to actually achieve the planned goal. Any performance gaps, experienced or created, result in the need for *process improvement.*

Focusing our process improvement on measurable gaps in performance to define problems does two things for us as leaders and for our facilitators and teams. One, it takes the emotion out of the situation. If we focus on measurements, the definition of a problem becomes inherently objective. The "walking-around sense" of "everyone knows this is a problem" or "it happens all the time" or "they never do it right" is quantified and compared against a baseline or benchmark. You can more effectively evaluate the magnitude of the problem, and from that its relative priority to resolve.

Second, it takes the focus off the people and puts it onto the process. This is perhaps the most important principle for problem-solving. That the operator is not guilty.[17] If the people executing the process are an apparent cause for any defect, we must look deeper. Too many times I have seen "retraining" as the countermeasure to an identified problem. Telling your people again with the same communication or training program may, at best, only have a temporary impact.

At the core, process problems are often capability problems. Leadership needs to have more introspection and understand how their system allowed someone who was not capable enough to run a process make that mistake. We should look into how we define and control those processes, evaluate if the tools used for the job are sufficient, and determine whether the hiring process or onboarding/training for the task was insufficient.

---

17 Michael Ballé and Freddy Ballé, *Lead with Respect: A Novel of Lean Practice* (Lean Enterprise Institute, Inc., 2014).

Nobody wants to come to work and make mistakes, and, generally, people want to do a good job. Blaming the people executing the process is a cop-out for management and puts the guards of the team right back up. Folks are more conscious of not messing up than they are in looking for what can be fixed. In this mentality you can be assured that fewer problems will be pointed out in that environment, because people don't want to be blamed!

As you gradually show more respect for your people and front-line value creators, then you'll uncover more opportunities for process improvement. Improvement is achieved when we "close the gap" on the problems that have been identified. Improvement is what drives our business or organization forward. Improvement is what links our strategy deployment to the daily management of our operations. Improvement is neither leadership's job alone, nor is it relegated to frontline employees. As a critical element of the business system, it needs to be understood and executed at all levels.

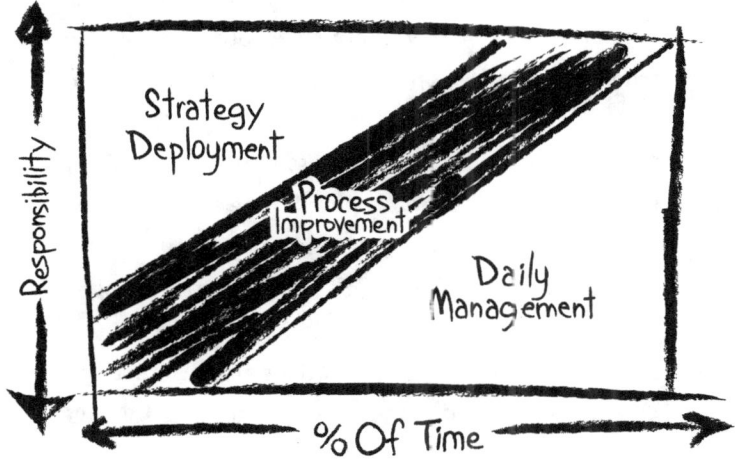

Figure 3.2: Business Management System

Most leaders in business got to where they are because they were good at solving problems. They turned around a department in a crisis or led the business through massive growth or were the go-to person for firefighting and troubleshooting. That leader may have a natural bent for scientific thinking, and they likely have their own internal process for breaking down and analyzing problems. But the power for an organization comes in multiplying that problem-solving capability. Going to one or a handful of resources in your organization for making decisions or solving problems becomes a bottleneck for growth and development of the workforce.

A quick word about problem-solving versus troubleshooting:

Troubleshooting is when you resolve an isolated event that may not have impacted performance or results. One example is when a shipment arrives early at your facility and you need to stage material until staff has time to move it to a warehouse. Another example is when IT deskside support resolves a user's access issue.

Problem-solving is addressing systemic or recurring issues. From the previous example, one early shipment can be resolved with troubleshooting, but if we have a string of early deliveries, there is a deeper problem to resolve. Likewise, troubleshooting a single user's IT access is one thing, but a deeper configuration problem may need resolution if we repeatedly have issues in the department.

Moving into leadership positions should pivot the responsibility from solving problems to teaching how to solve problems. Imagine the speed of execution and the explosion of untapped potential in your organization if the cadre of problem solvers increased.

To teach and replicate structured problem-solving based in scientific thinking, you need a common method. Codifying problem-solving and improvement into your business system is the platform to teach, coach, develop, and . . . ultimately . . . multiply your capabilities and results.

Problems come in a range of complexities in business. Regardless of complexity, it is beneficial to leverage simple, underlying methods to resolve those problems by managing the approach rather than the complexity of every unique problem. We do this with common problem-solving methodologies.

Overall, most problems you encounter in business are relatively simple. Using a relaxed but common approach is what we will refer to as a "Just Do It" problem. More complex issues, due to the nature of the problem or organization dynamics in change management, require structure to ensure resolution and cross-functional adoption. In either situation, the thinking follows a framework known as DMAIC, an acronym that stands for the five phases of problem-solving: Define, Measure, Analyze, Improve, and Control.

This problem-solving methodology was made popular by the Motorola Six Sigma program in the 1980s. Each phase of the method builds progressively to refine the problem and justify the solution, ultimately ending in a process change or control to prevent reoccurrence. As a phased approach, there are qualitative criteria to "complete" each phase and move on with the problem-solving effort. These requirements keep the individual leading the effort, their team, and impacted stakeholders aligned. In addition, both categories of problem (JDI or project) can be resolved in an expedited fashion as a problem-solving "event" when the priority and urgency of the issue warrant. This will be discussed at the end of the chapter.

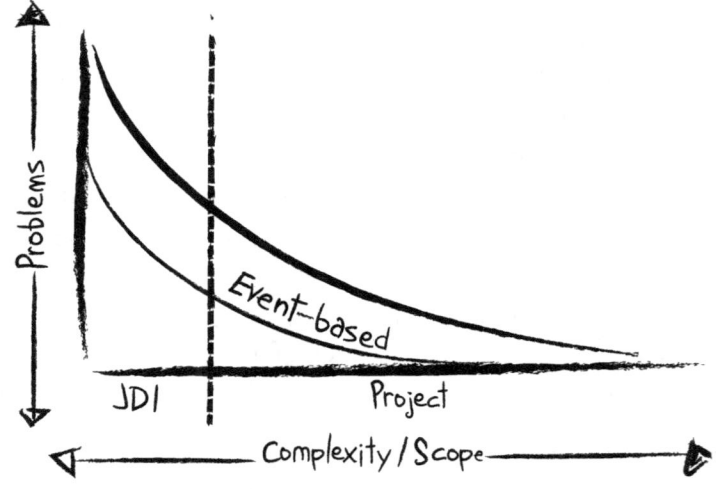

Figure 3.3: Problem Distribution

DMAIC Methodology

Problem-solving should be thought of as a funnel, a narrowing of focus to an eventual root cause and solution. Focusing our effort is beneficial, because when your problem definitions stay too broad, the team cannot get to specifics and ends up trying to address multiple issues with one solution. This narrowed vision allows us to surgically address the root to the symptom rather than shotgun blast the process or uproot it altogether.

When the team does not focus on a specific point of cause and associated driver, the changes are broad and vague, making it difficult to claim effectiveness. This mindset of breaking the problem down and addressing the component parts sequentially is at the heart of continuous improvement, as it implies that there will be a next step, a next improvement to follow. For more information on some of the tools referenced in this section, see Appendix I: Resources.

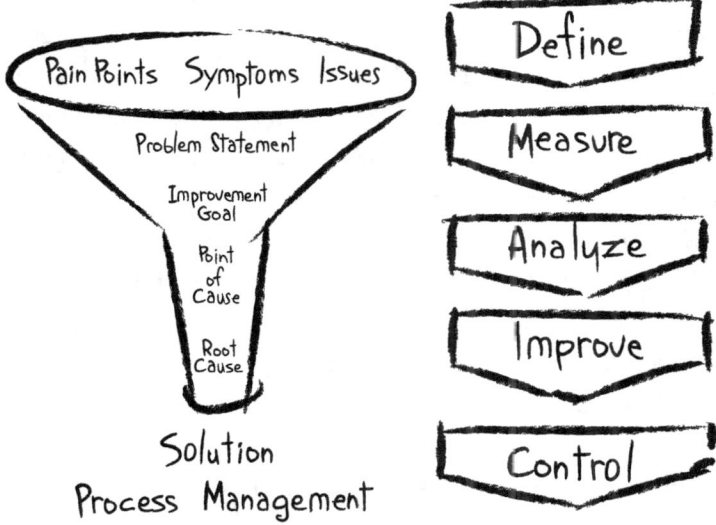

Figure 3.4: Problem-Solving Funnel

Define

The first step in improvement is to define a problem to resolve. Resolving the problem will help close the measurable performance gap. In this phase of improvement we seek to answer three questions about our initiative: (1) What is the problem? (2) What is the process? (3) What are the requirements/constraints?

For the problem we use the "gap" image in Figure 3.1 and the SMART guidelines for a problem statement: specific, measurable, attainable, relevant, and time-bound. *Specific* constrains the scope of the problem to a facility or production line or product variant or service offering to effectively bound the scope of the analysis and solution. *Measurable* establishes the magnitude of the problem for prioritization and ultimately quantifies if the problem has been solved at the end of the project. *Attainable* is an improvement target that is meaningful to the business but also realistic for the team to accomplish. (In some cases the target is already established as a standard or historical benchmark that needs to be achieved.) *Relevant* implies that the problem affects KPIs for the team or downstream customer. *Time-bound* establishes the period of performance when the degraded performance occurred or the deadline for implementation of the solution and improvement.

I spend time on this topic because a poorly defined problem is a leading cause for ineffective problem-solving or unsustainable solutions. If the team can be clear on the problem they are facing, everything flows effectively from that foundation.

To understand the process we visualize the process flow through a form of process mapping. There are a variety of tools to visualize a process. The critical element here is to get the current state of the process documented so everyone on the team and applicable stakeholders can agree on the sequence of operations and known pain points. This could be a flowchart, swimlane diagram, routing analysis, or value stream map. An agreement on what the current state of the process is as well as the perceived pain points is needed to focus the team during the next phase and measure the contribution of each driver / point of cause.

Finally, the team needs to understand requirements. Downstream internal resources or the end (external) customers may have constraints that the solution must meet. Those could be physical size or interface requirements, software or electronic system integration, cost, or lead time for implementation. We obtain this information by identifying and communicating with the relevant stakeholders through interviews, focus groups, surveys, or direct observation. Gathering and confirming those requirements with stakeholders is valuable for building awareness for the potential change and constraining the solution so it fulfills customer expectations. Once there is an agreed-to understanding of the problem, the process, and the requirements, the team is ready to move into the next phase.

Measure

The second step of improvement is to measure the actual process execution and determine the goal for this initiative. We seek to answer two questions in this phase: (1) What is the point of cause? (2) What is the potential for improvement?

Although the "gap" of the problem may be, say, 15 percent on first-time quality (implying we have 15 percent more issues than planned to manage), there may be several drivers behind that issue. To establish a goal for improvement, we break down the problem as contribution by parts. There are common tools in descriptive statistics and graphical analysis to segment the problem and focus on the largest contributing factors. Those include histograms and pareto charts and pie charts, to name a few. The intention is to narrow the focus to a subset of factors, or else the analysis and solution are too broad to implement quickly and measure their direct effect.

After separating the causal factors for the problem of focus, the team needs to isolate which issues and steps in the process are in scope. We call this the point of cause. The intent is to continue moving down the funnel to a specific driver and associated root cause. Focusing in on which types of defects or causes we are investigating also allows the team to narrow scope for the step in the process to take into the analyze phase.

It is important at this step that the problem-solving team "go see" the actual process being executed and confirm that the problem is occurring as you understand it, at the process step you claim. With the team aligned on defining the problem and properly measuring the impact and contributing factors, they can move on to analyzing the root cause.

Analyze

The third step for improvement is to determine the root cause and a potential solution. We seek to answer two questions: (1) What is the root cause? (2) What is the solution concept? Being aware of the point of cause and the target for improvement, it is now desired to understand how the issue occurs.

Beneath every apparent cause is a root cause. The intent is not to address symptoms (like cleaning up an oil spill) but rather to identify and eliminate the root cause (repairing the leaky hydraulic line). The complexity of the problem may necessitate different process knowledge, technical skills, and tool usage.

The art in knowing how to investigate comes through repetition and coaching. Yet there are some simple quality tools that are time-tested to aid us in this search. Qualitative tools such as cause-and-effect (or fishbone) diagrams and 5 Why analysis provide logical relation between the causal factors evaluated and the specific problem at the point of cause being evaluated.

Again, the team or leader should "go see" the process to confirm the relationship between the proposed root cause and problem occurrence. Statistical tools can benefit the team here to analyze and visualize historical data or design an experiment to show correlation between the problem and process control settings. Numerous texts and resources exist on these topics/tools, so we'll introduce only the concept and typical application.

With the root cause confirmed, the team has reached the bottom of the problem-solving funnel, the specific issue that needs to be prevented or remediated. It is on to proposing a solution. Oftentimes there is sufficient process knowledge on the team that a solution is obvious. It could be changing a process setting, rearranging steps, changing physical location, or fixing a nonconforming piece of equipment.

If the root cause does not have an apparent solution, teamwork is required. Benchmarking of other areas that do not have this issue, literature search for documented solutions, or brainstorming are common ways to ideate potential ways of resolving the issue. The team must coalesce on the "best" solution. There are tools available to aid in prioritizing from a list of options. The team now arrives at a proposed solution to the hypothesized root cause, at the prioritized point of cause, to close the gap in the problem statement. They must now plan to test and verify the effectiveness of that solution.

Improve

The fourth phase is to demonstrate the improvement. We are required to answer two questions at this phase: (1) Have we achieved the improvement target? (2) What is the new process or product?

After moving through the first three phases of problem-solving, we arrive at this point where we verify our solution will remedy the hypothesized root cause and achieve the expected performance improvement.

This is our threshold of knowledge about the process. We know and have observed all the data and events up through the analyze phase. We don't "know" that our solution will work. We "believe" it will work based on what we have learned; hence it is important to be structured and logical in the prior stages. To verify the improvement and provide evidence in support of change management for the organization, it is incumbent on us and our problem-solving team to demonstrate that with evidence. Through verification testing we need to show we have closed the performance gap reflected in our problem statement. At times a full-scale implementation of the solution is not feasible due to cost or complexity, and confidence needs to be provided before that investment.

It is possible to prove the concept through a prototype, pilot run, or simulation. The obligation is to show that the change, the solution, mitigates the targeted root cause from occurring and achieves the process improvement. A level of confidence in the solution helps create a platform for change management. Affected stakeholders should understand the changes required (any new tools, new sequences, or new information) in their process and how they interface with it. Those changes are to be captured and documented to establish a standard that can be taught and managed. With scope of change needed and solution concept proven, it is time to move onto full implementation and control.

Control

The fifth and final phase of the DMAIC improvement methodology is to scale up implementation to full scope and put controls in place to sustain results. We are required to answer only one question: How do we plan to sustain improvement?

Robust problem-solving for improvement is intended to deliver a long-term solution. For any process change to "stick," there have to be controls in place to ensure the process continues to operate as designed.

Many of you may interpret "controls" as micromanaging. These are not for leaders to control the workers but rather for the workers to control their process. Controls include things like standard work (documenting the safest, highest quality, most efficient way to do a job), as well as workplace organization (5S program, see appendix), visualization of the workflow and performance (tier review boards) for awareness and adjustment, or mistake-proofing techniques to design the error out of the product or process.

You may choose to implement formal checks or inspection points to verify you are meeting design requirements or customer needs. Controls should be developed *with* the employees performing the work so they are empowered by the tools, not shackled by them. And control also implies the leadership behaviors required to reinforce process execution with their teams. This handover of the solution from "project" to ongoing "process" needs to be managed with the key stakeholders in the business. Leadership needs to navigate this and reinforce the use of process controls. Positive coaching of personnel back to standard and explaining why it is important are incumbent upon frontline leadership.

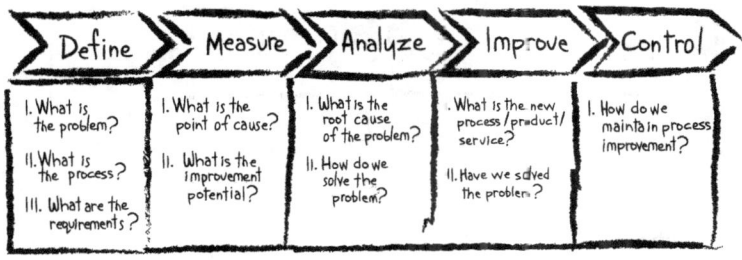

Figure 3.5: DMAIC Process Improvement Methodology

Just Do It

When the problem is common or well understood, when the root cause is presumably known and a solution is available, we can move through the DMAIC method informally, using a "Just Do It" approach to problem-solving. The DMAIC thinking should still be present, as it aids the team and their leadership by writing down their thoughts, ideas, and attempted solutions.

We use a simple one-page template to document our thinking and learning through the problem-solving process and results. Often we do not document our thinking and experimentation in business problems. But forcing ourselves to be disciplined about writing down our investigation, our hypotheses, and our expected outcomes enables collaboration and coaching during the activity, as well as learning for the team after the effort is complete.

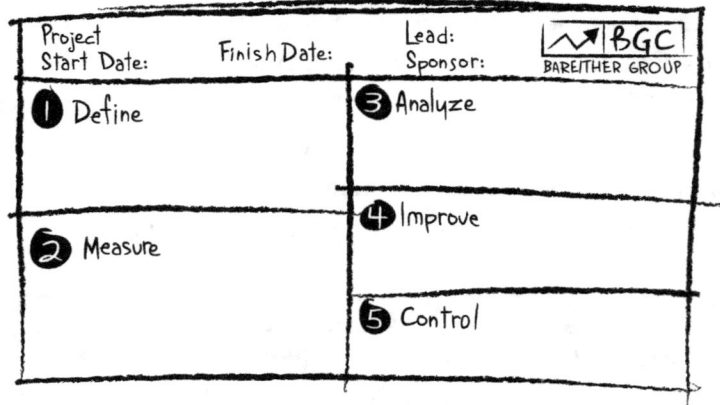

Figure 3.6: One-Page Summary Template

Each phase has an allocated section. The team should include text, pictures, sketches, and tools used to answer the questions of each phase as a storyboard that explains the change and verified results. It should be done in real time as the team is investigating the problem rather than a post hoc documentation exercise. Writing down the problem-solving activities builds the capability of problem-solving and allows the leader to better coach and critique the team on their thinking and tool usage.

Over time, familiarity with the methodology, tools, and this template make the process fluid and efficient. I have walked teams through the DMAIC process and documented the problem and results in as little as thirty minutes. And it is not about the tools. If this template does not work well for your team, modify it or find one that does.

Templates are just tools . . . like an instrument to a musician. When you are first learning to play the instrument, any one will do. Once you settle into your style and sound, you may look for a tool that better matches your playing and physicality. That's okay. But we must not abandon the thinking framework of the DMAIC method. Though we "just do it" and solve the problem, we should be able to trace a logical flow backward from the control to the demonstrated improvement, the analyzed root cause, the measured impact at point of cause, and ultimately the defined problem.

Problem-Solving Project

More complex issues are pursued as projects. Due to the resources required to solve or the functional boundary handoffs that need to be managed, coordination and alignment of resources is needed to implement and sustain a solution. As changes to a cross-functional process may have consequences elsewhere, we engage impacted stakeholders to ensure that proposed solutions are feasible and trade-offs are a net benefit for the company.

The application and flow of the DMAIC methodology remains

the same; however, it is encouraged to document the initiative in a charter and review the scope and progress at completion of each phase to keep the effort aligned. Problem-solving (or process improvement) projects should be owned by the functional sponsor of the effort and hence managed in their own daily management system (discussed in chapter four).

While subject matter experts or coaches or consultants may be used to support the team. The portfolio of improvement projects should be owned out in the business. After all, the problem resolution is improving that line of business's capability to deliver better results on their KPI tree.

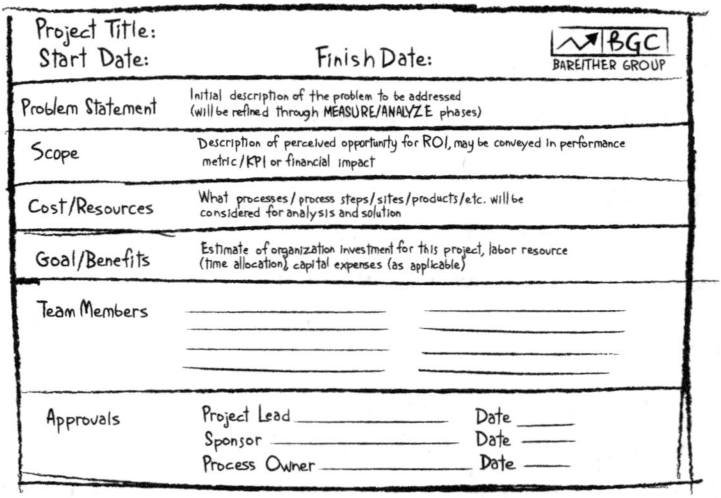

Figure 3.7: Example Project Charter

Throughout the process improvement project execution, impacted stakeholders should be aware of a change happening. Change management is incorporated within each phase of DMAIC.

The ADKAR® model developed by Prosci[18] is an approach that nests neatly alongside the five-phase DMAIC method. It stands for awareness, desire, knowledge, ability, reinforcement.

During each phase of the problem-solving method, we also bring stakeholders through the change curve with us. In the Define phase we make relevant stakeholders *aware* that we have identified a problem and are evaluating a process change. Next, in the Measure phase, we update our scope and business case to show the potential improvement and create a shared *desire* for the change. The Analyze phase drills to root cause and potential solution, which builds the *knowledge* of why the problem is occurring and how we need to change.

As we test and verify the solution in the Improve phase, we build and identify gaps in *ability* to execute the new process. As we complete the Control phase, we reinforce the change with training, process controls, and leadership behaviors. Ending the "project" of making an improvement dovetails into daily execution of the "process." Naturally, the business management system element of daily management follows. After we develop or improve a standard process for the business . . . we need to manage it.

---

18 Jeffrey M. Hiatt, *ADKAR: A Model for Change in Business, Government, and Our Community* (Prosci Research, 2006).

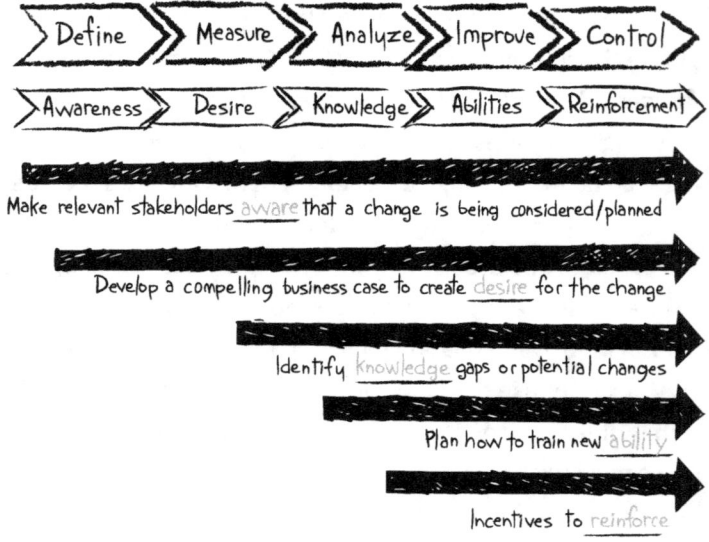

Figure 3.8: DMAIC & ADKAR

Problem-Solving Event

At times the priority or urgency of a problem may necessitate dedicated resources to resolve. In this situation, the DMAIC problem-solving methodology can be implemented in a structured event. *Event* in this connotation implies that it is a finite period of time with full-time resource allocation. Depending on the scope or the issue, the event may span one day or up to four weeks. For illustration here a common one week problem-solving event is described. This could be scaled by proportion to the time required in each phase for simpler or more complex issues.

Preparation work is needed to narrow in on a problem definition before the event. The event lead or facilitator should define the problem and an organizational goal for the event. This will include alignment with stakeholders before kicking off the event.

This should be intuitive, since you will be asking those stakeholders to free their people to participate.

Day 1
With the problem defined, the event kicks off and begins with an overview of the event schedule and training on any of the basic tools planned for application. Then the problem definition and scope are reviewed with the team as well as any requirements/ constraints gathered from stakeholders.

Day 2
The team collects data from the process (ideally direct observation and measurement). Time, quality issues, and variations in process are documented as they pertain to the problem statement, and the team agrees on the point of cause and improvement goal for the event (intent is to meet or exceed the planned goal).

Day 3
The team analyzes the issue and plans how to fix the problem. By the end of the day the team should have a proposed root cause, a potential solution, and all logistics planned to test the solution on day four.

Day 4
The improvement is verified by testing the solution. This could be a prototype or pilot of the new process, but it must show resolution of the root cause, which the team can relate to the improvement goal.

Day 5
The team reports out what was accomplished and gets endorsement

for implementation. The one-page summary shared earlier is a great storyboard for these events. Stakeholders should be scheduled to participate in the live report to show support, endorse the changes, and celebrate with the team. Ideally changes can be made that afternoon. For longer lead activities the implementation plan should begin.

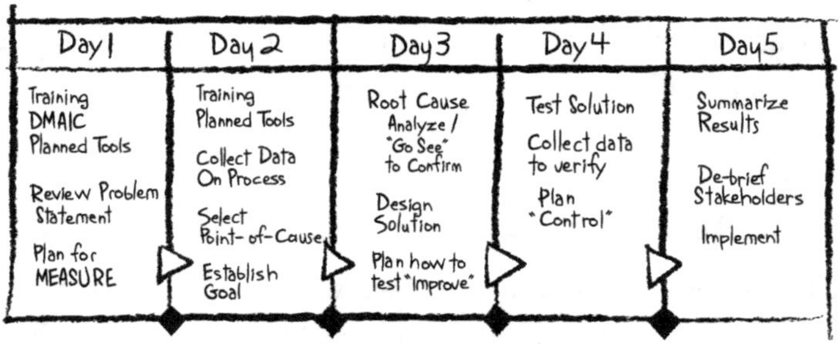

Day1	Day2	Day3	Day4	Day5
Training DMAIC Planned Tools	Training Planned Tools	Root Cause Analyze / "Go See" to Confirm	Test Solution	Summarize Results
Review Problem Statement	Collect Data On Process	Design Solution	Collect data to verify	De-brief Stakeholders
Plan for MEASURE	Select Point-of-Cause	Plan how to test "Improve"	Plan "Control"	Implement
	Establish Goal			

Figure 3.9: Problem-Solving Event

Problem-solving is process improvement. By addressing issues that have degraded the current state or leveraging an opportunity to raise the performance bar, we are making strides toward the strategic goal we set for the organization. More stable, predictable, and efficient processes are easier to manage on a daily basis.

No matter how good you get you can always get better, and that's the exciting part.
–Tiger Woods

4 Daily Management

THE ENGINEERING DIRECTOR IS hurriedly stuffing his belongings into a backpack to move on to the next meeting. He pulls his lunch out of the bag to make room for his laptop. "I haven't even had a chance to put my lunch away," the director tells me, chuckling.

"I know," I think to myself, concerned after bouncing around between meetings and ad hoc conversations to gather information on daily issues and identify priorities that need to be evaluated. From 8:00 to 11:30 a.m. this was the pace, and I was not completely sure what the day would have in store or who would need to be consulted to make decisions and assign resources until lunchtime.

"*Seems like a pretty nonstandard morning,*" *I state with a questioning tone.*

"*No, this is pretty standard,*" *he replies with a sarcastic smile.*

But does it have to be? Is this the system we want to operate the daily business, or can we structure and simplify daily management?

Fast-forward a few months. At a daily site review the leadership team is poised and ready to report escalations and receive information from other departments. They know their intent for the day and have set plans and priorities. Process KPIs are reviewed at the designed cadence of meetings from front line to plant level. Any measure that is offtrack is discussed and an action assigned to contain or resolve.

"*We're worlds ahead of where we were two months ago,*" *the director tells me in a coaching session. "The information and actions are flowing to [me]. I can see what's at risk and understand what we're doing about it.*"

Exactly!

—

A process is a sequence of tasks, or actions, that transforms an input to an output. That could be changing your raw materials into finished goods, your customer request into service delivery, or data into information. A foundational concept of continuous improvement is to look at every aspect of your business as a process. All value that our businesses provide to clients and customers has an underlying process, whether we have it well defined or not.

When we bring people together, connecting them as a team around a defined set of process performance targets, that is process management. To sustain and improve performance of a process, we need to treat our processes as an asset. Measure it. Monitor it. Manage it. Daily.

Measure it implies that we need to define how to measure the execution and results of a process. Monitor it implies that we need to report those measures on a consistent basis. Manage it implies that we need to make decisions and take action based on what we learn from measuring and monitoring. Daily implies that, regardless of how long a process takes, there is a step in our processes being executed every day. By actively monitoring the inputs and activities, we ensure consistent and improving outputs, or results.

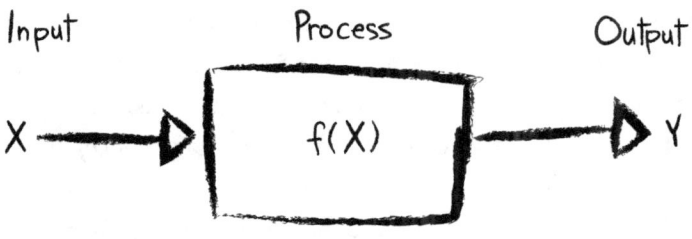

Figure 4.1: Process Diagram

Daily management is reporting and sharing information on the process performance and risks to make decisions on a routine schedule. The departure from classical management is that this review of performance is done with the team doing the work, not only the leadership. The team evaluates what they expected to happen, say a performance target or specification, and what actually happened during the prior period (shift/day/week). Recall from chapter three that this is the foundation of problem definition—measuring a gap between our target results and actual results.

When there is a gap, the team moves into problem-solving to resolve and stabilize. Leadership's role in daily management shifts from a review of metrics in a conference room and opaque decision-making, to discussion and coaching with the team executing the work.

Inherently, leadership cannot review every process, every day. That is where a system of these structured reviews helps to quickly funnel information upward and get leadership mobilizing resources to the biggest risks or challenges at hand. This is necessary to remove the time burden of the routine review meetings from leadership. Putting a system in place enables teams to be self-directed and focus on the processes and results important to strategy delivery. This does not absolve leadership of accountability for performance, or for teaching and coaching others. But it does drive responsibility and the ability and authority to make process decisions closer to the value-added work of the business.

If senior leadership becomes tied up in management of the daily execution of the business, it constricts their capacity for long-term thinking and action on strategy deployment and improvement. To get this time back as a leader, a system of information flow is paramount. Rather than relying on ad hoc disruptions to the day, this structure and schedule creates confidence for leadership to know *where* and *when* to get information about the business. For your teams, there are clear deadlines for communicating or providing updates. This predictability in reporting and decision-making frees time and keeps the entire team informed.

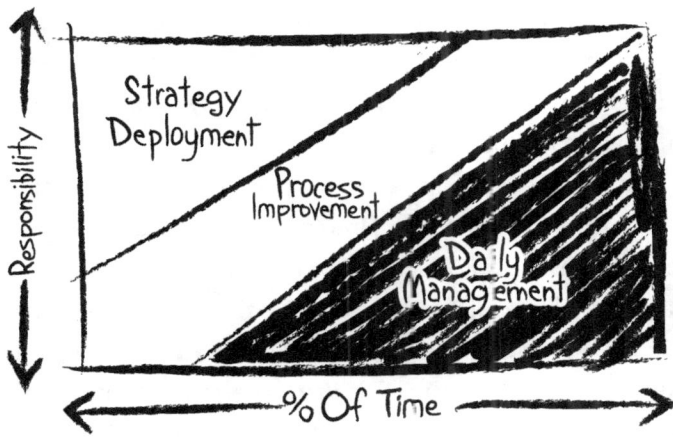

Figure 4.2: Management Element of the Business System

Daily management has a variety of names when applied within an organization: huddles, tier reviews, stand-up meetings, operating reviews. Regardless of what we name the practice, there are underlying best practices that need to be present: (1) having a balanced set of metrics to measure our process, (2) making our performance visual, (3) following a defined information flow, and (4) creating cycles of learning.

Balanced Metrics

What should you measure in a process? From the KPI tree structure built in strategy deployment (chapter two), the cross-functional leadership team identified the processes and evidence that needs to be managed to achieve performance goals. These are the minimum management requirements for the organization, the processes and metrics that need to be managed on a regular basis to ensure delivery of the top goal.

Your organizational structure, roles, and responsibilities

determine where each of those pieces of evidence are created and captured. We deploy those metrics to the responsible team, the ones doing the work, and start with this set of parameters to confirm on a routine basis.

Verifying execution of daily tasks makes the process output for the organization predictable. However, a process can be measured in more than one way. Each team or function may identify other measures that are important to balance the focus. If we choose to optimize on quality alone, it may subordinate delivery or incur additional cost. If we try to optimize on delivery, we may subordinate quality . . . or incur additional cost. And so it is important to choose a balanced set of metrics for a given process or team. A common set of KPI categories are Safety, Quality, Delivery, Cost, and Morale (SQDCM).

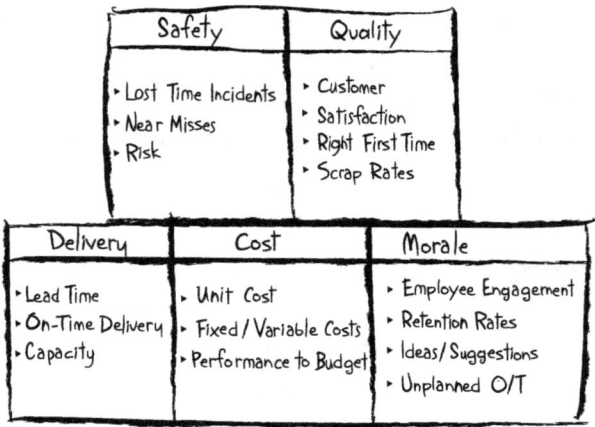

Table 4.1 Examples of SQDCM Metrics

You do not need a metric in each category to effectively manage your process. But it is valuable to keep a cross section of these measures in view for the team so they can learn to understand the impacts of their work across the "board." Here a "scoreboard" is implied. Much as the scoreboard at a sporting event gives immediate information to the status of a game, a team's performance board should give instant information on the status of their underlying processes.

It is not a requirement to measure a metric in all categories, so begin with the minimum management requirements from your strategy deployment KPI tree. Then balance your scoreboard as you learn about the process and what has impacts on the output. The format of the board (electronic v. physical) and the level of refinement (handwritten v. formatted) is not the most crucial decision. What is important is making sure that the measures accurately represent the stability of the underlying process and the impact on next-level KPIs. That leads us into the second best practice: make it visual.

Make It Visual

Running a business and reacting to daily variations takes information. Making performance and issues visual enables more transparent and faster communication of process information. Most information transmitted to the brain is visual, and visuals are processed almost twenty times faster in the brain than text.[19,20] This is why you need to make performance of these processes visual.

Process management visuals should also engage the team to leverage their creativity in how to display their metrics. Process management visuals should be accessible by all members of the

---

19 Anne Trafton, "In the Blink of an Eye" (MIT News Office, January 16, 2014).

20 O. Hauk, M. H. Davis, M. Ford, F. Pulvermüller, and W. D. Marslen-Wilson, "The Time Course of Visual Word Recognition as Revealed by Linear Regression Analysis of ERP Data" (Neuroimage, May 1, 2006), 30(4).

team, especially during daily review meetings. To evaluate the effectiveness of your process management visuals, you can reference the 1:3:10 standard. That is, in one second you can determine the status of a process (whether it is on target or offtrack). In three seconds you can determine any trends: How long has it been off target? Is it off target and improving? Is it on target but degrading? In ten seconds you can identify the cause and what action is being taken (the understood root cause, what is being done to correct performance, who owns the action, and the due date to report back).

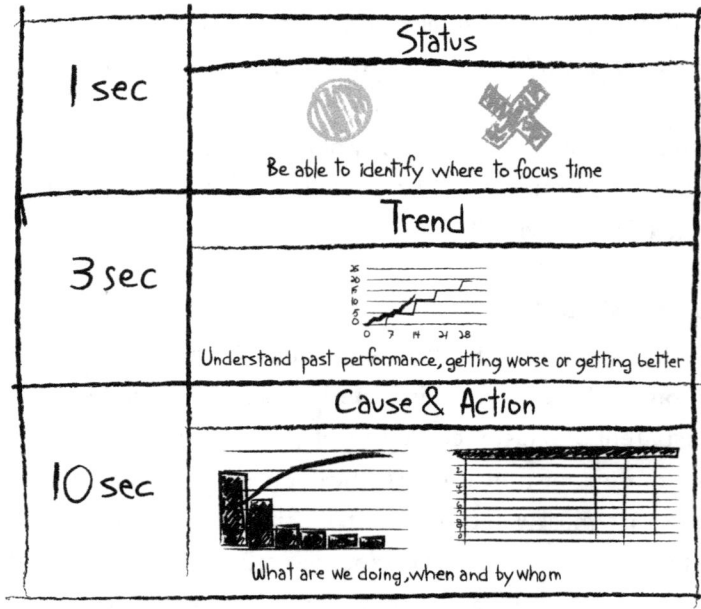

Figure 4.3: Example of KPI Visual Meeting 1:3:10

A minimum status category would be on track or offtrack (green v. red). As dictated by the sophistication of the process and needs of the team, status may get more complex through behavior charts or statistical process control. The key bit is that the team knows when to take action. And this is an important behavior aspect of performance boards: we shouldn't look at red as bad or punitive. Instead, we think of red status as a stop sign. We stop and think. Do we understand why the performance is off track? Do we know what we plan to do about it?

The first step is knowing when something needs to be changed. Trends and causes help the team have appropriate information to make decisions on these questions and move into action items. Observing the action item status informs us if the team has capacity in their day to address performance. Past-due or unverified action items indicate a lack of priority or bandwidth to address issues. Having all this information visible enables leaders to have a full picture of the team and process to coach and support.

Defined Information Flow

The most critical thing a leader needs to run their business on a daily basis is information. To make decisions and deploy resources, one must be aware of what is happening right now. This should not be constrained to only results. Results have already occurred. As teams learn more about their processes over time, they can identify potential issues and risks that need to be addressed and prevent disruptions or poor performance.

To enable this, a defined cadence of review meetings is established. The cascaded KPIs establish the standard for what must be reviewed every time. During the review the team looks back over the past period of performance (shift/day/week) and identifies any results or plans that are off track (that is, red). Action is taken to contain and resolve the issue at their lateral level of the organization. However, if the team is unable to resolve the issue with their knowledge, capabilities, or resources, it is *escalated*.

Escalation means we are notifying the next level of leadership that we were unable to contain the issue and it may impact results. Escalation promotes awareness and should come with a specific request to provide resources for assistance. The scope of escalation should also include a look forward over the next operating period (shift or day). Any risks are identified and addressed with the resources at hand. Escalation is used if the team does not have a reasonable mitigation for that future risk. To reinforce this thinking, begin with a standard agenda and format for your daily meetings and a sequential flow of daily meetings to transfer information.

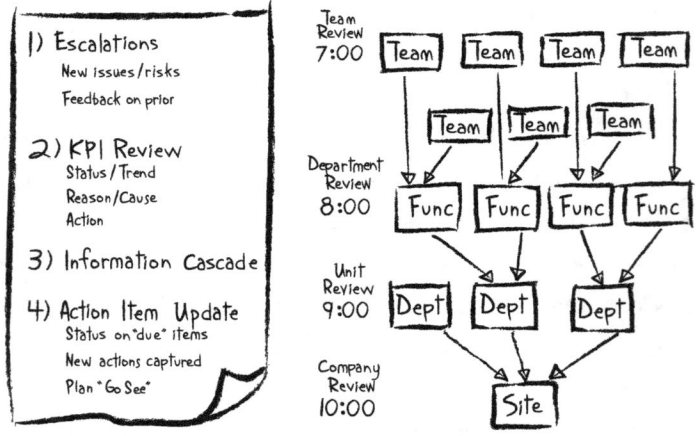

Figure 4.4: Example Standard Meeting Agenda and Site Meeting Schedule

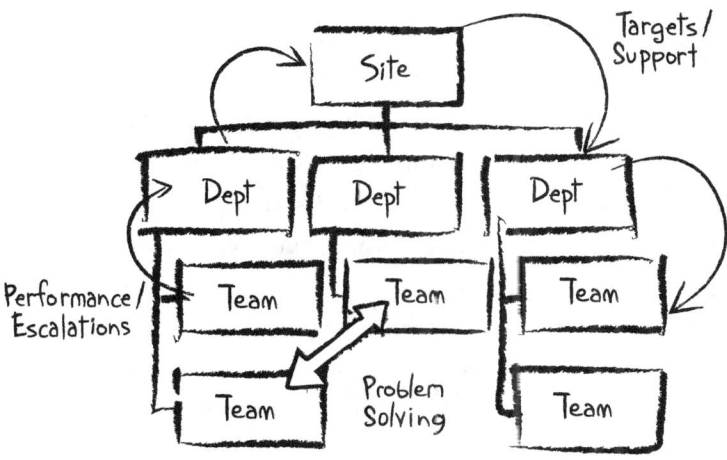

Figure 4.5: Tier Meeting Structure for Information Flow

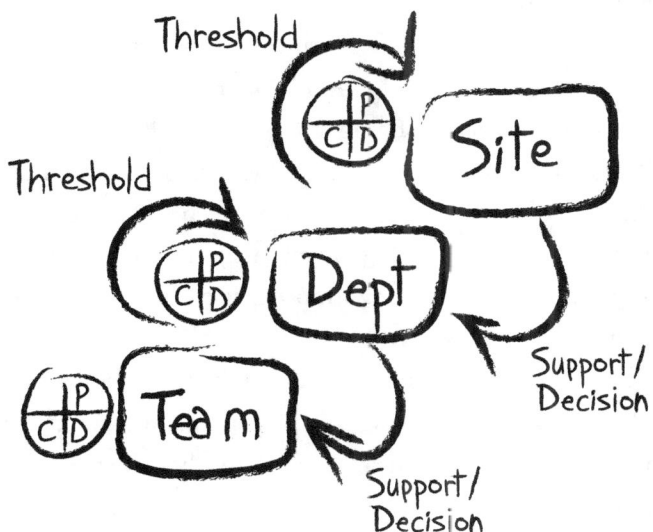

Figure 4.6: Escalation Process

Many organizations struggle with the flow of information. Establishing your daily priorities is difficult when you are unsure what problems will occur and when you will find out. Whether it is due to lack of understanding or a lack of trust, information flow is often an ad hoc process. The discretion of the team, based on tenure or capability, determines what a "problem" is and who needs to know about it.

Leaders attend as many meetings as possible because they want to be informed, because they are unsure if they will actually hear about the issues. Establishing a planned cadence of reviews with a standard agenda and clear expectations for reporting and escalation makes the flow of information constant and predictable. Leaders know when they will hear about issues, and teams know when they are expected to provide follow-up or hear updates.

Most issues, as a rule of thumb about 80 percent, should begin to be resolved at the level they are identified. So issues identified at the frontline may be found and resolved without the next level of leadership even hearing about them. This is not to hide issues or control information. This is to free the next level of leadership for more strategic thinking. (Leadership should be verifying and reinforcing this behavior with process confirmation, and there will be more on this later.)

Having clear expectations and autonomy empowers the team to develop problem-solving capabilities and own their processes. Thresholds for escalation can be explicit where there is significant operation impact. As shown in Figure 4.6, a threshold for time down on a production line may trigger escalation as it is a precursor to a delay. As leadership matures in their management of the business requirements, the team also understands their process and capabilities better. The clarity of knowing when to ask for help and what processes and KPIs are of priority to cover on daily management frees time for the entire organization for the investment of short daily reviews.

Cycle of Learning

In the 1950s, Dr. W. Edwards Deming introduced a four-phase approach to process management and learning, described by the phases Plan-Do-Check-Act (PDCA).[21] The cycle of learning in its thinking way is reinforced or systemized by a daily management system. We *plan* our activities and expected results. We *do* the work that was planned. We *check* our results against the target or plan. We *act* on any deviation from expected results.

Repetition builds this scientific thought process over time. The team and their leadership become better at identifying risks in advance and adjusting plans. As you pivot from management of results to management of activities . . . the results follow. Across the organization there is a deeper understanding of how changes in a process or input affect the output (results).

The thinking way of PDCA overlapped on the daily management cadence sets the table for effective coaching of next-line leaders. We can use Socratic questioning to build awareness and competency. The leader and the team are conditioned to the expectation that they come to a review or escalation with the problem AND a perceived cause AND a proposed action AND what they expect will happen.

---

21 https://deming.org/, accessed September 27, 2022.

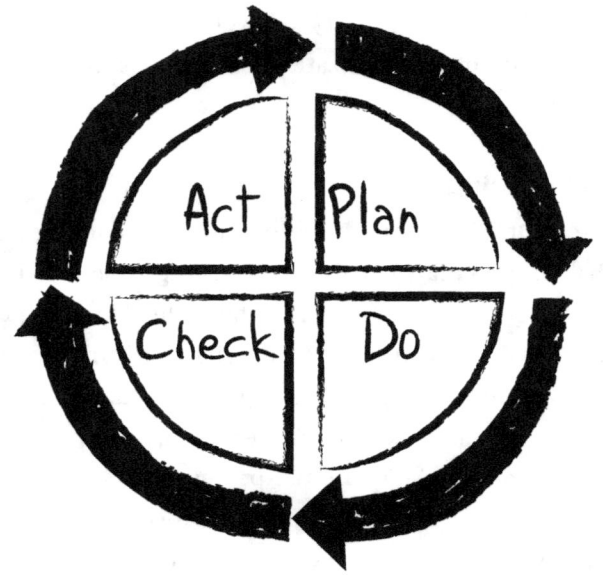

Figure 4.7: The PDCA Deming Cycle

These four aspects of a daily management process come together to form a cohesive system for managing your business on a recurring basis. Building capabilities and responsibility closer to where the work is performed speeds up decision-making and frees leadership to focus time on strategy deployment and improvement. With balanced metrics and transparency of performance, the teams are better informed and hence knowledgeable in how the processes are performing.

The clarity of reporting and escalation builds confidence in the team and their leadership about information flow to keep the business moving forward and to know where to allocate resources. The business requirements deployed through the strategic goals and KPI trees in chapter two outline those priority metrics.

Cross-functional teams are aligned on what is important and

how and when information is shared. Leadership reinforces the value of this process-based thinking and reporting over time by "going to see" next-level review meetings and following up on actions to address performance issues and escalations. Team competency and leadership value in a daily management system is a foundation for sustainable continuous improvement. This is the type of continuous improvement that will outlive changes in leadership or team turnover because this is simply *how* we run the business.

Process Confirmation

If we pull our perspective back and look at the entire business system, we are able to see how the three elements of strategy deployment, process improvement, and daily management interact and culminate in this routine cadence of confirming the most important processes and metrics.

Strategy deployment outlines and cascades priorities in terms of key processes and KPIs. Where we are offtrack from target to achieve our goal, there is focus on process improvement. The metrics and KPIs that will lead to realization of goals are controlled in a daily management cadence.

Numerous organizations have leveraged this system of elements to stabilize their business for sustainability and scale. One such organization that I supported had daily management implemented across all functions of the business. Each day led off with a review of performance and any known risks. Those could be unplanned absences, equipment maintenance, shipment delays, or quality concerns. Problems or risks that could be managed at the identified level were, and others were escalated for awareness or help.

The first review was held at the start of shift (7:00 a.m., for example); then three tier reviews at next-level leadership followed. At each level of escalation most of the issues were decided upon or resolved. If a first line leader could resolve the issue cross-functionally with their peers, it was done so and not escalated.

Soon all risks and priorities that had broad impact were known, and plans to "go see" or make a decision were in place. The predictability of information flow freed leadership time to engage in longer-term planning as the teams became more mature in managing their own processes and solving their own problems.

In the next chapter we will walk through the five-step framework to begin operating like this in your organization. This role of responding to escalated risks and also routinely observing processes to reinforce adherence to standards and problem-solving thinking is the role of leadership. At each level of the organization there are people to be developed and processes to be confirmed. Leadership's responsibility is to engage with their people and reinforce processes, maintain standards to get predictable results, and develop problem-solving skills when we don't get what we expect.

Just think of business as a process.
—Colin Bryar

5 Implementation

*"THESE AREN'T EVEN THE metrics that are import-
ant to me!" claimed the department manager.*

*We were months into strategy deployment,
ready to start monitoring monthly performance
and managing related activities, and now ... NOW
she was telling me this.*

*I learned a lot from that engagement. One lesson
is that "the effectiveness of communication can be
measured by its outcomes." If we ended up in the
situation, together, then I owned at least half of
the accountability.*

*It was apparent that the bigger picture had been
lost. In this department we had lost the forest for
the trees and were plodding along using the tools
but not changing behavior or performance. Some
of the best lessons are from our mistakes. There*

were two key takeaways from that experience. One, overcommuni-cate during any change. If you think you have said it enough, say it again. The second thing I learned was that you need a clear process to guide a transformation. Even if you're doing all the "right things," doing them in the "right order" and the "right way" is important. The process keeps the organization aligned and accountable to what has been agreed to.

In the second iteration, things were a little different.

"This is great. This makes a lot of sense, and it is exactly what we need."

We had a process, and that took away the uncertainty and clar-ified expectations. When the organization collectively knows where they are going, how they are going to get there, and what they will measure to determine progress, they have alignment.

—

A lot of organizations want to improve. Some organizations get to that point of view on their own terms. Others are driven to improve out of necessity, whether that's related to pressure from competi-tors, evolving customer needs, changes in industry or regulation, or new technology. Regardless of internal motivation or external driver, a critical starting point to any continuous improvement transition is to understand "why" you are doing it.

The framework laid out in this book will help you to successfully deploy the tools presented here and build your business manage-ment system. You may already have some of the components in place—great! As you move sequentially through the process, you may need to realign some of the elements and tools that are already deployed in your organization. The details can be referenced in the chapters that precede each step.

The process is simple but not always easy. Stick to the process and tools that are provided. Over time you may discover tools or templates of tools that work better. Cool! What has been presented here is a standard that will work for most clients. The start of deployment is like the first time you pick up an instrument. It doesn't matter much what guitar you buy when you start learning. As you advance, you gravitate toward a guitar, a "tool," that matches your style and the style of music you play. So noodle around with the tools, but stick to the process. As you learn what works or what you need, feel free to expand or augment. Let's get into the process.

Figure 5.1: Business Management System and Process

Step 1: WHY—Define the Vision

There are three components that define the lens through which an organization views the world and itself. Those are a mission, a vision, and a set of values. When shared across leadership, it creates that common lens that can focus and align the organization to pursue a shared vision of the future. This may sound a bit woo-woo for strategy deployment, but it is a necessary starting point.

Use the mission and vision worksheet to facilitate the conversation with your top-line leaders. Synthesize the information gathered into a mission statement you can all nod your head to and a vision statement that inspires you to stay on track for the next four steps of deployment. The clarity of organization mission and vision (WHY you exist) enables the team to align on objectives and goals (WHAT you want to accomplish).

These measurable milestones mark the path toward a future that is aspirational for your organization and your customers/ clients. There can be a lot there, so I recommend you start with *just one* objective. The process is scalable for organization size and complexity, and the process is repeatable. So, after building some muscle memory but moving through the process once, it will be easier to pick up additional facets of your strategy later on.

Figure 5.2: Mission, Vision & Values

Step 2: WHAT—Establish Objectives & Goals

After choosing an objective and associated goal that is crucial to "get right" in the next one to three years, build the KPI tree to define the system. The KPI tree ensures that leadership across functions and departments understands the goal and what it will take to get there.

The first layer of decomposition entails the requirements to deliver/produce the goal—what situations, conditions, or status needs to be true to deliver and achieve the measurable goal. Cross-functional participation is important here to capture fringe thinking and have everyone see the problem from all department viewpoints.

The next layer entails the key processes that deliver those requirements. There are defined or ad hoc processes that create the conditions described in your requirements layer. Understanding across the company the processes that deliver the requirements needed for success clarifies shared priorities—the kind of improvement that lifts the system, not simply optimizing a department's performance.

The final layer entails the activities or metrics to measure and manage in your key processes and controls that are in place. These are the tangible things your leadership team closest to the work can see and measure on a regular basis. The structure of the entire KPI tree represents the management requirements to achieve the goal.

The management system you are building defines the activities to monitor every day. You will not have to improve or manage everything on the KPI tree right away. Start with where you can agree there is variability that needs to be brought under control. Only with stability can we sustain and eventually scale performance. The system of accountability and responsibility for processes and KPIs becomes the backbone for the flow of information and escalation of issues in your daily management.

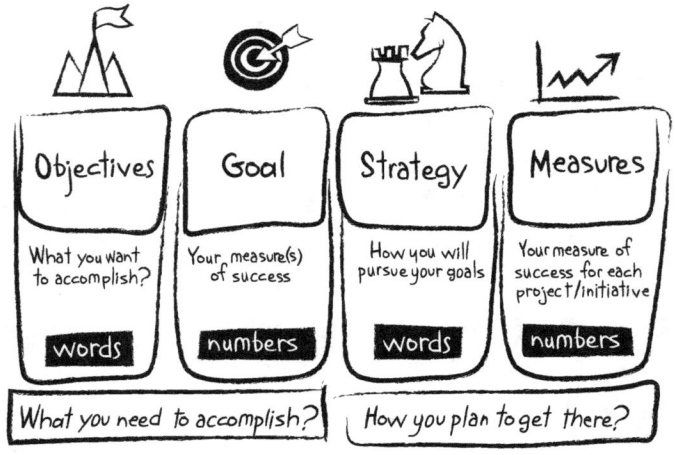

Figure 5.3: OGSM Definitions

Step 3: HOW—Identify Targets and Improvements

Every department or team in your organization is likely not the same size or structure. Depending on the org structure, the deployment of management requirements and improvement responsibilities will fall to differing levels. The layers of the KPI tree are cascaded to the appropriate level in the organization where that process/ work takes place.

For leadership to understand where those processes and metrics reside is helpful to routinely confirm the management system in place. The established system requirements create information channels to manage disruptions rather than react to poor results. As discussed, these management requirements can be vast, so it is best to prioritize your focus and deployment of process management.

Where do you *need* to improve or stabilize? There are always daily tasks to execute and daily disruptions to manage. Managing the right ones takes insight and experience. Management of the established requirements is allocated to specific teams. They will be responsible for monitoring, reporting, and correcting performance. A need to improve performance may already exist. The need for improvement can easily be seen through the KPI cascade and measurement. Where we have a gap in performance—that is, actual performance does not meet target performance—we have a problem to solve. And so this cascading of requirements to the responsible part of your team establishes the expectation for daily management and the accountability for delivering improvement.

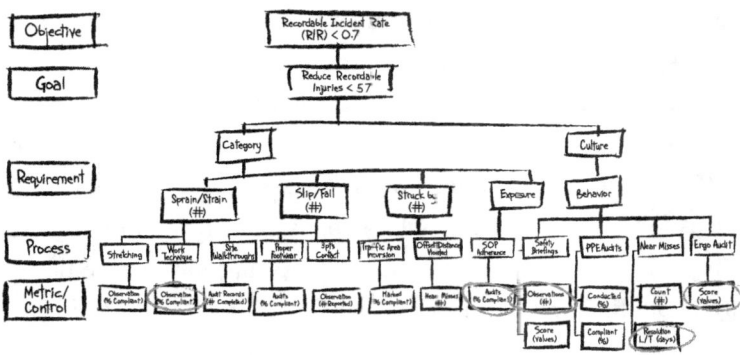

Figure 5.4: Identify Where Evidence and Processes Are Managed with KPI Tree

Step 4: WHO–Cascade KPIs to Manage

Ownership needs to fall to an individual. I want to be clear on this point. Most problems are system or process related, not people related. The "owner" in this regard is accountable for reporting status and facilitating improvement. The intent is not to have someone to blame. It is to be clear about who is collecting the data, diagnosing the problem, and problem-solving or suggesting actions. Process ownership goes hand in hand with KPI ownership. The individual held accountable for reporting performance should also have enough authority to change the process when the performance is offtrack.

In some situations correcting performance may be a simple action for a well-understood cause. Other times the required improvement is beyond what we have achieved before or the problem is not well understood. Now is the time to engage with problem-solving. Where the gaps in performance occur, we must correct that exception to be confident our goal will be achieved. Teams work to close those gaps and stabilize performance using the DMAIC methodology of problem-solving.

Defining the problem is now simple. We know what we expect in order to achieve the KPI at the top of the tree. We know what is currently happening by the metric or process confirmation. The difference, the gap between where we are and where we need to be, is the problem we are looking to resolve. The team now maps the processes and identifies stakeholders that would be impacted by a potential process change. Problem defined.

Moving into the measure phase, the team collects data at the process level pertaining to the problem statement. Process takes too long—measure how long each step takes. Process is poor quality—measure where and when mistakes are made or found. Process costs too much—measure the cost contributors.

Focus in and decide which process step or component part you are focusing on first. Improving that will narrow, or even close, the performance gap. Understanding where to focus is crucial to analyze the cause of the problem at that step. Now the team digs into that process step through observation, interview of experts performing the job, or data analysis to decide on the factors that most contribute to the problem *at that point of cause in the process*.

Sharing what you have discovered with stakeholders is important before developing a solution to gain alignment and ensure you have not missed something. Now it is time to experiment. Test out a potential solution or solutions to evaluate if you can eliminate or reduce the issue at the point of cause you selected. This may be done through prototyping, pilot runs, or simulation. The data for your experiments should confirm or reject your solution as effective. *Note: you may need to iterate here to get an effective or an optimal solution.* Eventually, with a proven solution in hand, you need to control the process change. The progress and associated performance are monitored in the daily management system you put into place.

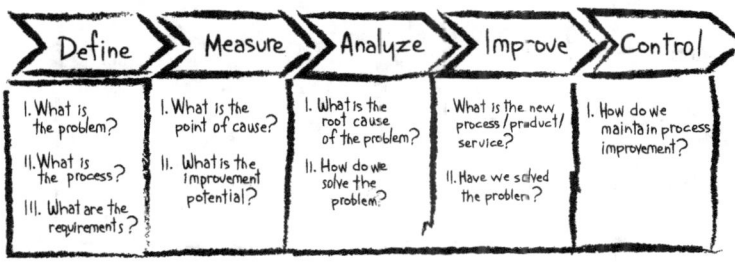

Figure 5.5: DMAIC Process Improvement Methodology

Step 5: WHEN—Daily Management to Sustain

With management requirements in place we don't simply throw the organization in cruise control and dust our hands of it. The work of leadership is to create accountability and coach the team. On a regular and recurring basis, you verify that processes are being executed correctly and the team is getting results they expect.

Where the standard process was not followed, we point them back to the standard and explain why. Where the process was followed but we don't get the results we expect, we ask why and coach them through the problem-solving method. Then repeat. This becomes the standard that leadership follows to reinforce the value of standards at each level of the organization.

As you move further from the front line of value delivery, less of the work is repeatable with fixed inputs and fixed outputs. The daily management element is made up of the standard work for the workforce at that level of responsibility. Leadership confirms the processes they are responsible for and creates accountability for the next level of leadership, closer to the work, by confirming their processes.

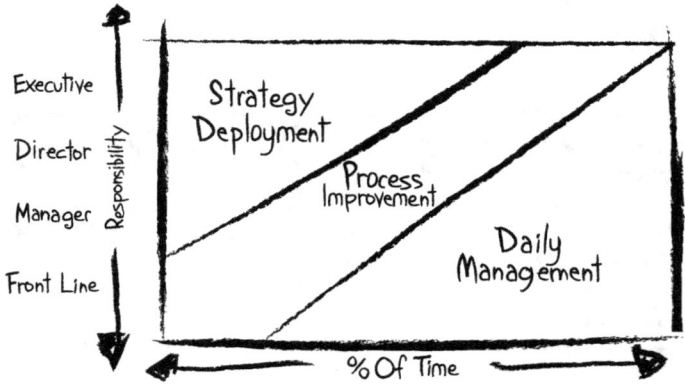

Figure 5.6: Business Management System

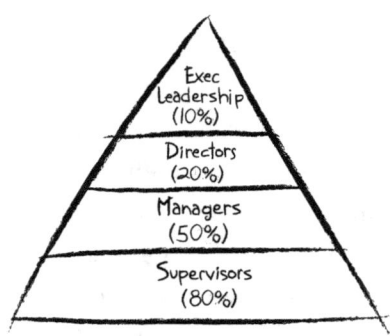

Figure 5.7: Guideline for Percentage of Time on Process Confirmation

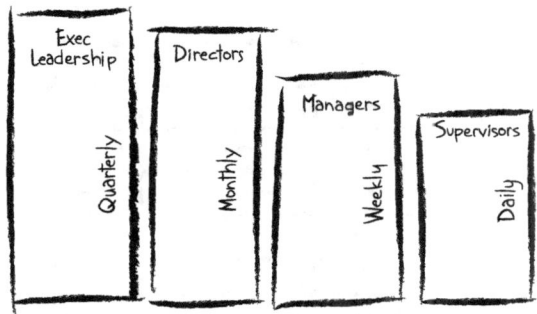

Figure 5.8: Guideline for Cadence of Process Confirmation

The tool serves to reinforce the activity and behavior when confirming processes. The activities that should be confirmed are tied back to strategic goals through the KPI tree and management requirements. Processes or activities that take place within my span of control as a leader should be confirmed at a regular interval to ensure understanding, execution, and development of problem-solving.

As opposed to hoping or intending that I check up on these things, Leader Standard Work plans when the follow-up should occur. As perhaps the most important job of leadership in delivering the management requirements, time needs to be planned to observe and coach. Leader Standard Work can be managed in various formats and templates. To illustrate the concept, a template is shown as an example of how the application of this concept can be realized and tracked. Leader Standard Work includes both the routine cadence of daily management performance reviews attended and process confirmation for tasks owned by the leader or that directly impact their results.

Leader Standard Work for _____					Week of _____	
Daily Tasks	M	T	W	Th	F	Notes
Staffing (Call-Ins)						
Scrap Review						
Action Items Due						
Coach Problem Solving						
Audit Time Cards						
5S Spot Check						
SOP Spot						
Lead Tier II Meeting						
Weekly Tasks	M	T	W	Th	F	
Audit Call Standard Work						
5S Scoring						
Audit Inventory Levels						
Safety Check						
Tier I Meeting						
Monthly Tasks	M	T	W	Th	F	
Review Key Projects						
Improvement Follow-up						
Strategy/Update						
	✓-Completed	X-Incomplete		O-Issue Found		

Figure 5.9: Leader Standard Work Template

A final word of advice here: simplicity is preferred. There are limits on our capacity. Measuring and reporting on metrics takes people's time. If managing our processes takes on more burden, it leaves less room for improvement and strategy. What are the critical fewest things you can monitor that also enable you to achieve your goals for safety, quality, delivery, cost, and morale of workforce?

Manage, but manage the right things. Choose what you want to deploy first. Then learn from those efforts. Check and act to iterate. If you learn over time that a particular metric or KPI in your management requirements is not important to the goal, use that learning to change the requirements or change the performance target. If you discover that the process is stable and doesn't require as much confirmation, focus your time and resources elsewhere.

You can add, subtract, and change as you learn through these cycles of PDCA. Improve LESS by focusing on the critical few items first.

One of the most important pieces of advice that can be provided is to *start*. There is rarely a "good time" to begin this journey. You will likely not find a lull in business or a calm period to dive in. Undoubtedly you will also not get it perfect the first time. Waiting for the perfect time or until you have the perfect system just means you'll be waiting. The framework outlined here and the tools provided are a starting point to build your business management system and get you moving toward your goals. It is up to you and your leadership to maintain the perseverance to consistently check and act as you make mistakes big and small.

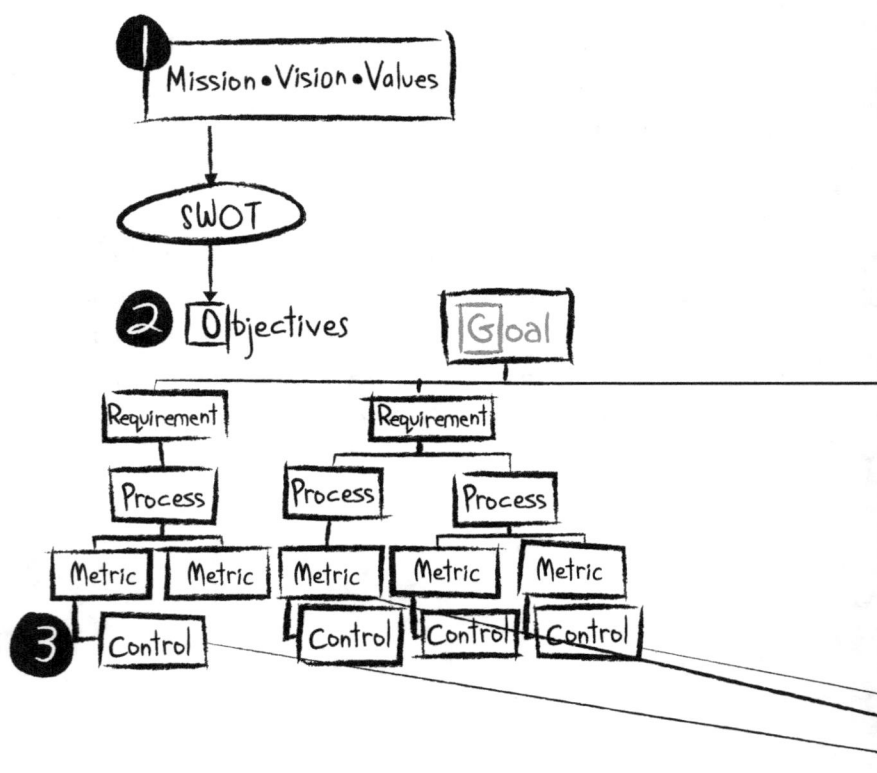

Figure 5.10: Focus and Align Framework™

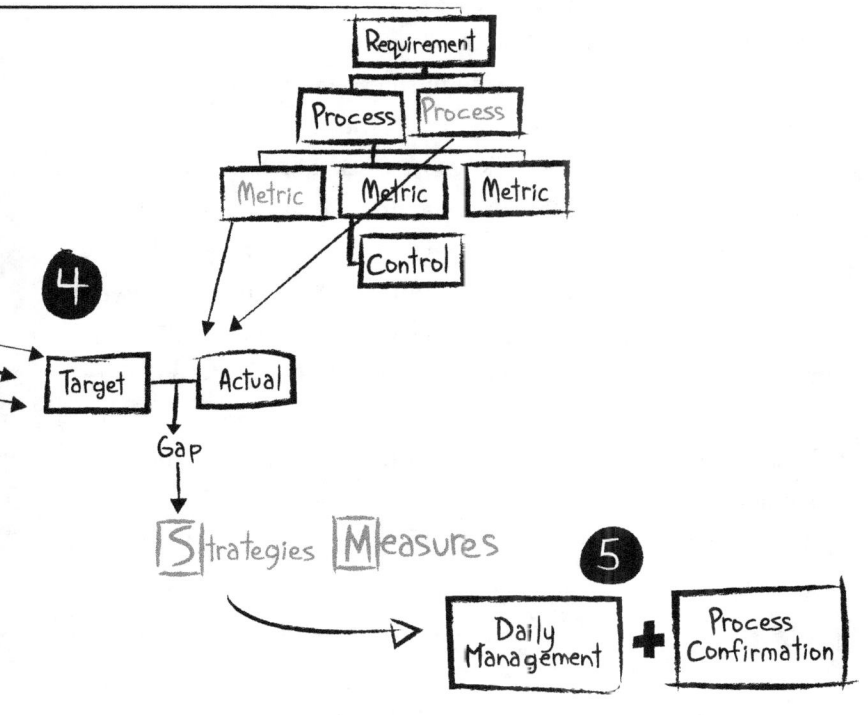

That's it. Deployment of the business management system follows those five steps of the Focus and Align Framework^{TM}. Every organization is unique. The combination of industry, age, maturity, sophistication, and resource availability all changes what elements of the system are already available and the pace at which you can move. Here I challenge you not to skip any aspects and try to complete them in order.

The rationale of the five steps answers the questions Why, What, How, Who, and When to build understanding and engagement of the leadership team and the frontline employee. The buy-in and alignment of your teams is what will enable you to achieve and sustain great things. Remember that the tools are not the important part. Modify or adopt tools to suit your business, industry, and maturity needs. The tools may change; however, the process is consistent.

And this may all seem like *more* work. Many organizations pursue continuous improvement as an additional initiative. The business management system promoted here is a change to the way you run the business. It is not something else you do; it is *how* you will manage the business. This is a change, and it does take time and effort. But I encourage you to see this not as a cost but as an investment. In the long run I see companies with more predictable days and weeks. I see leaders who control their calendar and don't live in their inbox. I see leaders who get their time back . . . and improve performance.

Failure is the most effective technique to optimize strategic
planning, implementation and processes.
—Thomas A. Edison

6 Leadership Behavior & Culture

I FOLLOWED AS THE vice president's arm slowly panned across the cityscape below. "That is our Gemba. That is our shop floor. That is where the work gets done." He was pointing at nothing specific but rather the rows of houses and businesses connected by visible utility poles and power lines and unseen natural gas lines. If I hadn't been invested in the vision before, I was now.

They were serious about transformation, serious about applying Lean principles to improve outcomes for their customers. The leadership commitment and behavior were aligned with the change they were promoting. It was the moment I decided that I HAD to work for this company.

As the old saying goes, the definition of insanity is doing the same thing over and over again but expecting different results. Change, improvement, was a choice. It was a choice to do things, to think about things differently. That choice came after awareness. Awareness of your current reality and awareness of where you want to go. This leadership team was there. They knew what they were asking was different, but that came from a place of awareness. Not only were they asking others to change, but they also changed—what they measured, how they planned, how they engaged with employees.

—

The sum of learned behaviors over time defines a culture. Culture becomes a way of life for a group of people. This could be for a geographic region, an ethnic group, or even your company. The behaviors and values that are demonstrated, or even tolerated, by leadership slowly cultivates the culture of your organization.

Studies have shown that most change initiatives do not deliver the expected level of results.[22] A contributing factor to this poor historical performance is leadership buy-in and reinforcement of the change. Total comprehension of the Lean or Six Sigma Body of Knowledge by leadership is *not* required to achieve desired results. Behavior and actions that align with the thinking are, however, *crucial*.

Choosing to focus on process improvement for your organization

---

22 John P. Kotter, *Leading Change* (Harvard Business School Press, 1996).

is an important decision. It will require *all* personnel to change. As a leader in your organization, the transformation is intrinsically linked to your commitment and your example. What you prioritize in your calendar, how you behave, and the type of questions you ask serve as an example and evidence of your commitment to the change. When an organization is growing or transforming to be more process-focused and continuous improvement–minded, looking back from the end state may inform some aspects from the start.

There are three primary outcomes from a consistent application of a structured business management system: higher customer satisfaction, better employee engagement, and more agility.

Customer Satisfaction = Focus on the Customer

The customer of any process is whoever receives the product or service you provide. Your customer can be an external, paying client, or an internal team you hand off to. You provide a good or service that your customer cannot provide for themselves; hence they are willing to pay for you to provide it. An internal resource may "pay" for this through investment in that department as a cost center or their time, waiting for you to do your work. The value placed on your work is defined by the customer, whether internal or external. Understanding what your customer needs is important to ensure your processes deliver—that is, to ensure you deliver on the expected time frame, at the defined quality level, at an agreeable cost, without compromise to your company safety or employee morale. This implies that we need to know who our customer is and engage with them to understand expectations.

An entire book could be devoted to customer engagement and translating requirements. To simplify here, you gather feedback by engaging with your customer through interviews, surveys, or direct observation of the end user. This outlines what the customer needs and expects from your product or service. Integrating this into your business by establishing a target for performance that meets competitive standard/advantage for those requirements is the baseline to measure your delivery. This approach to daily management was discussed in chapter four.

As your organization matures their processes and you better understand what the customer desires or will tolerate, you can adjust your processes and the associated targets to better meet those needs. Promoting this mindset of customer focus throughout the organization aligns processes to the needs of the downstream partners and, eventually, the paying customer. As a common mindset it removes arguments on process attributes or targets when the team can step back and define it objectively through the customer lens. And while the "customer is king," we must be diligent to push back. Meeting internal or external customer expectations should never come at the expense of the organization values and pursuit of vision (see chapter two).

One note to carry forward from the discussion on customer experience is that your frontline staff has the biggest impact on the customer. Those closest to the value creation and delivery influence quality and customer satisfaction more than management, directors, and senior leaders. The way they do their work creates the environment for consistency and opportunity for improvement.

The frontline staff of an organization have more customer touch points and more reps in on key processes than the shared service department or engineer who developed those processes. Studies have shown that highly engaged workforces generate higher revenue than their peers and are more likely to succeed in the market regardless of industry.[23,24] Modern studies have also shown that feelings of empowerment increase employee productivity and effectiveness,[25,26] along with higher job satisfaction and reduced turnover.[27]

This makes a lot of sense when we stop to reflect that the value creators of our business should likewise be valued by leadership. While employee engagement does have a known correlation to productivity, the approach and programs put into place often feel disingenuous, as though they are simply a means to an end. Many an organization will state in a lip-service town hall meeting that "people are our most important resource." But when those resources question why we do things a certain way, they are often met with "because that's how we've always done it." A different type of engagement can be pursued, one where the employees are engaged in the productivity and success of the organization.

We find an example of this in the meteoric rise of Trader Joe's during the 1990s. Trader Joe's and their staff work constantly to improve its customer experience. They proactively seek and respond to their customer feedback.[28] When I say "respond," it should be noted here the differentiation between reacting and responding to customers. A reaction is reflexive; it is ad hoc to address the issue

23 ADP, "The Attitudes of Europe's Employees Are Changing Fast," Workforce View in Europe Report, 2019.

24 John Baldoni, "Employee Engagement Does More than Boost Productivity," *Harvard Business Review*, July 4, 2013.

25 Christine S. Koberg, R. Wayne Boss, Jason C. Senjem, and Eric A. Goodman, "Antecedents and Outcomes of Empowerment: Empirical Evidence from the Health Care Industry," Group and Organization Management (1999), 34(1): 71–91.

26 Gretchen M. Spreitzer, Mark A. Kizilos, and Stephen W. Nason, "A Dimensional Analysis of the Relationship between Psychological Empowerment and Effectiveness, Satisfaction and Strain," *Journal of Management* (1997), 23: 679–704.

27 Blake Morgan, "100 of the Most Customer-Centric Companies," *Forbes* (June 2019).

28 Vivek Jaiswal, "How Trader Joe's provides EXCELLENT Customer Experience CONSISTENTLY," Customer Think, September 2017.

with a customer so we can get back on with our day. Responding takes time to understand the need and what would need to be true of processes or capabilities to satisfy that request.

At Trader Joe's, they want to understand the need and their processes, but then they will move fast. Team members directly interact with customers and have been known to alter the store layout or products stocked based on feedback. Team members are hand-selected in their robust interview processes for their personality and integration with the Trader Joe's culture. This customer-first mindset offers the ability to create the experience their customers want.

This focus on customer experience has worked well. Between 1990 and 2001, the number of Trader Joe's stores quintupled, and the company multiplied its profits by tenfold.[29,30] What would this look like for your organization? If you structure your processes around delivering the best experience for the customer, it will be felt in the loyalty of your base and your people.

Employee Engagement = Respect for People

Once your company grows to the point that you need coordination of the work, that implies a layer of management. A manager monitors the people and performance of a particular function. Chances are that even first-level management does not directly engage with the customer on a regular basis or personally deliver your product/service. If value creation occurs at the "frontline" of an organization, we are putting a lot of responsibility on those resources, and they are due our respect for that delivery. Even when

---

29 Somer Anderson, "Trader Joe's Stock Doesn't Exist. Here's Why," *Investopedia*, October 2021.

30 www.statistica.com/statistics/562981/projected-sales-of-trader-joes-in-the-us/, accessed June 20, 2022.

a leader "grows up" in a specific function or department, they are often years removed from executing the direct value-added work.

The first behavior to demonstrate respect for people is to "go see" the actual work. It is tempting to dictate decisions or problem solve for our teams based on prior knowledge. This, however, runs the risk of not being aware of what is actually happening today and short-circuits the engagement and development of the team. Furthermore, it does not empower the team to solve their problem for themselves. This not only disengages but becomes a self-fulfilling prophecy where the team comes to the leader with all the problems, looking for answers or solutions.

When going to see the actual work, the leader should be observing and listening, not always directing. This is a change in behavior and a difficult one. A lot of managers ascended to their position by being good at their job as an individual contributor. Now their objective has changed, and it is to develop the team in their charge to be good at their job and eventually become the next leader.

Listening to understand their knowledge of the work and current issues creates a platform for situational leadership and development. Truly respecting your people implies a development plan for the team members. Not because the human resource department requires it, but because it is what is best for them, the processes they support, and ultimately the company.

Creating a clear development plan to help each employee know where to deepen technical expertise or expand understanding of the business process is showing respect by helping get them where they want to go. Building a transparent career path removes the mystique around promotions and establishes urgency for all leadership to be looking forward and planning for their own succession. This, in turn, makes it easier for you as a leader. With clear plans and opportunities identified, you know what to coach and mentor on when going to see the work in action or having one-on-one conversations with your employees.

Even in organizations with great customer service and engaged employees, many decisions need to be made daily. The typical human makes thousands of decisions per day.[31] If we subtract out decisions on what to wear, what to eat, when to sleep, and other personal decisions, we are left with a finite capacity for critical decisions to make on our business. The quality of our decision-making erodes throughout the course of the day and with mental exhaustion of choosing.[32]

Across an organization or team, decisions are typically made by a core group of leadership who are accountable for the results. Even small tasks that require just a few minutes to review and make a decision expend this finite resource and sacrifice efficiency when we mentally task shift. To get time back for leaders to focus their decision-making *on the business* rather than *in the business*, authority needs to be allocated across the span of control.

Span of control refers to the ratio of employees who report to a given manager. It is widely accepted that there is no perfect number in organizational design that would be consistent across industry and function,[33,34] though we can find recommendations and benchmarks that put the typical range of about nine to one.[35] If we could broaden our inclusion down even one more level, we

---

31 Frank Graff, "How Many Decisions Do We Make in One Day?," PBSNC, August 12, 2021.

32 Andrew Cohen, "Why You Should Limit Your Number of Daily Decisions," *Entrepreneur Magazine*, May 5, 2015.

33 Ashwin Acharya, Roni Lieber, Lissa Seem, and Tom Welchman, "How to Identify the Right 'Spans of Control' for Your Organization," McKinsey & Company article, December 21, 2017.

34 Tiffany McDowell and Don Miller, "Spans and Layers for the Modern Organization," Deloitte Perspectives, 2019.

35 Tiffany McDowell, et al., "Organizational Design: The Rise of Teams," Deloitte Press, 2016.

would expand the number of decisions made by nine times! That is more team members who know what the customer wants and needs, more leaders who can engage with their teams and build individualized engagement, and more eyes on the process to seek out incremental improvement.

It also frees more senior leadership ranks to focus on longer-term, more strategic decisions—the ones that we often "don't have time for." This empowerment of the workforce to support decision-making also reinforces employee engagement. When you are individually involved with or responsible for the decision, you are more engaged in the result. If you are more engaged and more responsible, you want to ensure it is the right decision for the customer you serve.

Apple regularly ranks in the top tiers of employee engagement. This comes as no surprise when we look to the mindset of founder and former CEO Steve Jobs. Mr. Jobs held a view that was heavily influenced by quality management pioneer Joseph M. Juran. He believed we should look at everything as a repetitive process, and to make that process better we have to take it apart and put it back together again. That the best people to do that work are the frontline of a company. That we should approach our business processes scientifically and question why things are done a certain way.

Authority, Jobs believed, should be vested in people. Rather than requiring people to ask permission of management to make a change, management should teach the organization how to measure and understand and improve.[36] This became core to Apple's business processes and their policy and approach to people. As time has proven, it was successful. Apple routinely leads its industry in employee engagement and productivity to the tune of over $2

---

36 Dr. Joseph M. Juran Collection, "An Immigrant's Gift: The Life of Quality Pioneer, Joseph M. Juran—Transcript" (1995).

million of revenue per employee![37,38] And while the world around them has seen voluntary employee turnover increasing, Apple has achieved retention rates as high as 81 percent.[39]

While there are benefits and perks of Apple employment that factor into this impressive result, the foundational beliefs of company founders and senior executives that the people have critical value in improving their processes is what keeps many of the 150,000+ employees staying put.

Agility = Learning Mindset

Greek philosopher Socrates famously said, "The more I learn, the less I know," implying that deepening knowledge exposes that there is always more to learn. This is an important behavior to model for our teams. Having a learning mindset means that we challenge our own knowledge to deepen our understanding of processes and results. It means that we don't make decisions based on assumption, we ask questions to understand, and we experiment.

A leader can demonstrate these qualities to their teams by "going to see" the actual process rather than making decisions from their desk or in a conference room. Being curious is a behavior that creates a culture that isn't driven by past performance and known solutions. It reinforces critical thinking and builds the behavior and capabilities for problem diagnosis, problem-solving, and innovation. All scientific thinking is anchored in this process of making an observation, asking a question, forming a hypothesis,

---

37 John Sullivan, "Talent Management Lessons from Apple: A Case Study of the World's Most Valuable Firm," http://www.ere.net (April 14, 2014).

38 https://www.statista.com/statistics/217489/revenue-per-employee-of-selected-tech-companies/, accessed June 20, 2022.

39 Stacey MacNaught, "What Everyone Can (and Should) Learn from Apple's Staff Retention," *Inc.*, May 5, 2016.

experimenting to understand, and then updating understanding from the conclusion. This is the underlying thinking to both the DMAIC and PDCA processes introduced in chapters three and four.

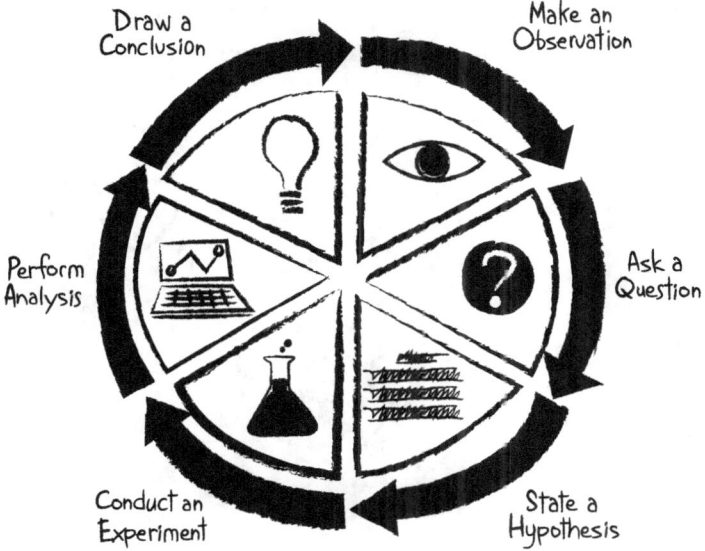

Figure 6.1: Scientific Method

The role of the leader is to coach the team members through this way of thinking. Does the individual understand what they are trying to achieve? What result are they getting? What is the next thing they can try to get a better result? What do they expect to happen when they make that change?

Link this back to respect for people by asking what support they need to take that next step. Then allow them to experiment and repeat your coaching cycle. This routine reinforces the learning process and the behavior of how team members should approach problems and ultimately coach/develop others.

Forcing ourselves to slow down and move through the scientific method of inquiry is essential for learning. If the claim is that we don't have the time to slow down and approach our improvements this way, perhaps we are trying to do too much. By narrowing our focus, we can have proper "form" and get good results. This format of coaching was made popular by Mike Rother in *Toyota Kata*.[40]

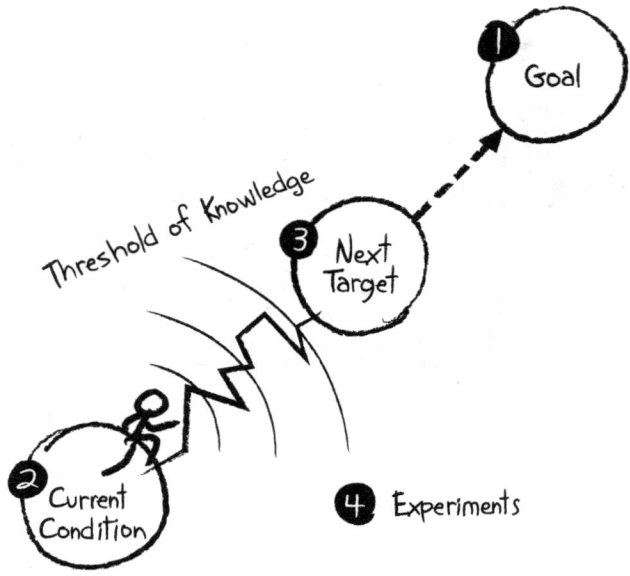

Figure 6.2: Kata (Form Training) Process

As leaders we are accountable to establish a system for managing the processes and making decisions. Giving the teams a framework to run the business and system to track and escalate issues puts them in the pilot's seat and frees you for air-traffic control.

Distribution giant Amazon has figured this out and uses

---

40 Mike Rother, *Toyota Kata: A Way to Practice and Develop Scientific Thinking in Everyday Work* (McGraw Hill, 2009).

processes to scale both capacity and human resources. Amazon thinks about its business as a process. They measure everything. Critical metrics are selected and defined as either controllable input metrics or output metrics.[41,42]

To do this they go through a process of experimentation to determine the controllable inputs and what settings yield the desired output levels. Do you think they are that deliberate and move at the speed they are able to with only upper management making the decisions? No way! By establishing a framework and a system to define and control their processes, they can empower the entire army of Amazonians.

That paradigm enables the management of processes while exploring new businesses and innovation on current products/ services. Amazon manages the layers of process through a weekly business review (WBR). WBRs are cross-functional, looking at an end-to-end view of the business, reporting out of performance values from the controllable inputs and outputs from each division or level.

This escalation of process performance and learnings also serves to cascade information and strategic decisions. We can learn a lot about how Amazon operates internally by what they promote through its Amazon Web Services (AWS) division. AWS even trains other organizations how to scale through process in a similar way. Process and process management has allowed the AWS team to work with an ever-increasing number of start-ups in a scalable way.[43] They, in turn, teach organizations and start-ups

---

41 Colin Bryar and Bill Carr, *Working Backwards: Insights, Stories, and Secrets from Inside Amazon* (St. Martin's Press, 2021).

42 Cedric Chin, "How Amazon Measures Itself," March 17, 2021.

43 Richard Howard, "Scale of Fail: How to Build Processes and Mechanisms the Amazon Way," AWS Startups Blog, August 16, 2019.

to define processes and metrics. To pull the owner and leadership up and out to focus "on the business" with a system that provides confidence for managing daily process execution while still keeping leadership informed.

But how did they get there? How did these organizations cultivate a customer focus, empowered employees, and learning mindsets?

Figure 6.3: Culture Soup

The culture you create is like the stock, the base of a continuous improvement "soup" you are making. If the base is off, if it is tainted by bad seasoning (bad behaviors), it doesn't matter what you layer on top it will still be gross. However, when leadership seasons it with respect for people, a learning mindset, and customer focus, it creates a brilliant broth as a foundation for the ingredients of your tools and systems and methods.

Tools and processes help to achieve improvement, but your culture and your business management system are required for stability and sustainment. Your unique cultural values (chapter two) also need to be supported. The behaviors that you define to support those values are mixed in alongside these uncompromisable continuous improvement ingredients.

Awareness

So . . . you've made it this far. You are still convinced that you want to lead your organization through a continuous improvement journey. You are committed to clarifying and deploying strategy. You are dedicated to closing your gaps in performance through process improvement. You will install a cadence of daily management to reinforce the system with information flow and action to achieve desired results. It is important to be self-aware of your own current behavior and discipline to following your system. It is a choice you have to make as a leader. The transformation is not something that is accomplished or sustained by all who endeavor.

Even Lean juggernaut Toyota Motor Corporation is open about sharing all their management approaches and systems and tools. They don't fear release of this information as a threat to competitive advantage. They are blunt about the fact that although these systems and processes are better, frankly "you're not going to do it." The rationale behind the statement is that the shift in management style and culture won't permeate leadership. You need to be leading this change from the top and being firm on alignment to the framework throughout the business.

You can't get there without feedback to consistently align with your values. Objective third-party feedback on what you are claiming to support and how your actions align with that message is eye-opening and correcting. Get a mentor or develop a personal board of directors to help you with this. Hire a coach or a consultant to hold you accountable.

In chapter two we covered developing your organization values. In this chapter we present three behaviors required to sustain continuous improvement. Having objective feedback is powerful and crucial in the early stages to reinforce the behavior change for you and your team. Also consider regular audits of your schedule/calendar.

In chapter one we discussed the leader's role in process confirmation of the management system and a tool to evaluate. A routine reflection on this should indicate whether you are spending the time to "go see" the critical process and KPI management in your organization. The motivation of your values and vision, along with the discipline of a management system, breed sustainable continuous improvement for your organization.

You can do it. Your first step is the most important one. Then stay committed in your thinking to being customer focused, developing your employees, and learning along the way. Narrow your strategic priorities to help yourself and your teams truly know where you are going and what is important. Get out there with the energy of an organization focused to improve LESS . . . but get better results.

Awareness precedes choice and choice precedes change.
—Robin Sharma

Appendix 1: Resources

THESE RESOURCES ARE PROVIDED *to aid you with independent implementation. It should be noted that building and maintaining a business management system based in continuous improvement is more about the behavior and thinking. However, tools and processes help create the structure to promote the "right" behaviors and thinking. Some digital templates of these tools are shared on our website at* **bareithergroup.com/templates**. *Start with a standard and modify or replace tools to meet your business needs.*

Chapter 1

Leader Reflection Worksheet: This worksheet is to promote self-awareness of where your time is invested on a daily and weekly basis. An honest assessment of where your time is consumed is a powerful setting for coaching and mentoring. Becoming aware of where you spend your time enables you to prioritize activities to delegate or delete from your obligations. This allows you to focus on the more value-added responsibilities of your role.

Chapter 2

Mission, Vision, Values Worksheet: This worksheet is designed to facilitate a discussion and alignment with leadership on the mission of an organization, the vision they are trying to realize, and the values that are important to maintain in that journey. Clarifying the purpose and why you have chosen to pursue continuous improvement is crucial for the entire organization to understand and align with.

SWOT Analysis: The strengths, weaknesses, opportunities, and threats analysis is a common framework to evaluate the landscape of your business and external influences. The process of conducting a SWOT analysis aligns leadership on a similar footing so they can plan where to go next. Input to the SWOT analysis can be gathered as a workshop or anonymously and synthesized for team review. The team evaluates the SWOT analysis against mission and vision to decide on what strengths and opportunities to leverage as well as which weaknesses or threats to hedge.

OGSM Worksheet: The Objectives, Goals, Strategies, and Measures Worksheet is a strategic planning framework developed by

ArchPoint Consulting. It has been deployed in multiple industries, so the versatility is broad. The benefit of the approach and the worksheet is to align leadership and quickly focus supporting layers of the organization to enterprise-level effort. This system-level thinking helps ensure that improvements made in functional areas of the business "add up" to business-level benefits.

KPI Tree: Key performance indicators (KPIs) are metrics that confirm directional alignment and progress for an organization. Often KPIs are results or outcomes. To manage by KPI, it is crucial to develop a management system of requirements, enabling processes, measures, and controls. The KPI tree achieves this decomposition visually so you can decide on the points of the tree worth managing or improving to achieve the top-level KPI goal.

Chapter 3

DMAIC: DMAIC stands for define, measure, analyze, improve, and control. It is a structured problem-solving methodology used in the Six Sigma approach for continuous improvement. This systematic approach is used to identify and eliminate process inefficiencies, reduce defects, and improve overall performance.

ADKAR®: ADKAR is a change management model that focuses on the individual and their ability to adapt to change effectively. It stands for awareness, desire, knowledge, ability, and reinforcement. This approach helps organizations navigate through change by creating awareness about the need for change, generating a desire to support it, providing the necessary knowledge and skills, enabling individuals to develop the ability to implement the change, and reinforcing and sustaining the change over time. This five-step approach pairs with DMAIC for process improvement to build change management into the problem-solving process.

Flowchart: A flowchart is a visual representation of a process or system using symbols and arrows to illustrate the sequence of steps and decision points. It provides a clear and concise overview of how tasks connect to help understand and communicate complex processes. Flowcharts are commonly used in various industries to identify bottlenecks, inefficiencies, and opportunities for improvement.

Swimlane Diagram: A swimlane diagram, also known as a cross-functional flowchart, is a visual tool used to depict the flow of activities and handoffs across different individuals, departments, or functional areas. It uses horizontal "lanes" to represent process participant responsibilities. They are valuable for identifying handoffs, clarifying roles and responsibilities, and improving communication and collaboration between stakeholders involved in a process.

Routing Analysis: Routing analysis is a technique used to optimize the movement of goods, information, or people through a system or network. It involves evaluating and improving the routing decisions and pathways to enhance efficiency, reduce costs, and minimize delays. By analyzing factors such as distance, time, and number of handoffs, routing analysis helps organizations redesign processes. It can be applied to logistics, supply chain, or internal transactional work.

Value Stream Map: A value stream map is also known as a material and information flow diagram. As implied by the name, it is a visual representation of how materials and information move in an organization to transform inputs into a finished product or service. Value stream mapping helps organizations identify and eliminate non-value-added activities or waste to optimize the end-to-end process flow.

Stakeholder Analysis: Stakeholder analysis is a systematic approach to identifying and understanding the individuals, groups, or organizations that have an interest in or can influence a project. By analyzing their level of influence and potential risks, stakeholders can be classified and prioritized for involvement or communication plans. Effective communication, engagement, and management of stakeholders minimizes resistance to change or project implementation.

Voice of the Customer (VOC): Understanding the needs, or sometimes constraints, of your customer is important to ensure your product/service meets their expectations. Likewise, it is important to know what these needs are when planning a change or improvement, to evaluate potential negative impacts. The "customer" can be defined as both the end user and consumer of your product/service. Internal "customers" also exist and may be the individual or department that you hand your product or information to for the next step in the workflow. There are different ways to solicit feedback on your process and their needs.

Interviews: Interviews are direct conversations with the customer or stakeholder. It is important to conduct interviews with the same questions and sequence to avoid biasing the responses. Though the most time-intensive method of VOC engagement, it enables you to ask follow-up questions and explore nuance of the response to planned questions.

Focus Groups: Focus groups are similar to interviews but are performed with a group of stakeholders/customers. This may be done to increase reach with your engagement or to get diverse opinions into one session to agree on common requirements. You must be careful to moderate strong personalities to give all participants a voice and defeat anchoring bias, where the first comment or idea constrains the group's thinking.

Surveys: Surveys can be administered digitally or on hard copy, and they can be done at the point of use or sent for remote completion. You are able to efficiently target a large population of customers/stakeholders with one effort. Two challenges to be aware of on surveys are (1) low response rate (at a typical response rate of 20–30 percent, you may need to send out five times as many surveys as data you need to analyze) and (2) question structure (to analyze the responses, you need to think about how the question is asked and the format of the response; this can limit your survey design, but do not think about how to analyze the data *after* you collect it).

Observation ("Go See"): A powerful data collection method is direct observation. Watching your customer execute their processes or use your product can be eye-opening to what you believed was happening. It is important to make those you observe aware that you are planning to observe them and the purpose of the visit. Collecting process data (for example, cycle times) can be supplemented with what you see occurring and asking for clarification from the users on what you see. Whether a problem with your customer or a problem in your business, leaders should leverage "go see" as a practice to move beyond assumption to a better understanding and knowledge of the issue.

Graphical Analysis: Graphical analysis refers to the practice of visually representing data and information using charts, graphs, or diagrams to gain insights and make informed decisions. By plotting data points, trends, or patterns on a visual medium, it helps individuals and teams understand and compare different variables. Common/standard types of graphical analysis exist that make it easy to comprehend what information is being communicated; these include line charts, bar graphs, scatter plots, histograms, Pareto charts, and pie charts.

Cause-and-Effect Diagram (Fishbone): A cause-and-effect diagram, also known as a fishbone diagram or Ishikawa diagram, is a visual tool used to categorize potential causes of a known problem or an effect. The format resembles a fish skeleton, with the problem or effect entered at the head and the potential causes branching out as bones. The main categories typically include people, process, equipment, materials, measurement, and environment. The fishbone diagram helps teams stimulate creative thinking to systematically identify the root causes of a problem.

5 Whys: The 5 Whys analysis is a simple yet powerful problem-solving technique used to determine the root cause of a problem by repeatedly asking "why" until the underlying cause is uncovered. By asking "why" repeatedly, teams can peel back the layers of symptoms or apparent issues to reveal the fundamental root cause. The analysis can branch at each progressive "why" question, but causes should be verified with data, observation, or expert opinion. The end nodes of the analysis represent root causes that support the development of effective countermeasures to the effect.

Descriptive Statistics: Descriptive statistics refers to the branch of statistics that involves summarizing and describing data sets using common numerical measures or tables. It provides a concise overview of the main characteristics of the data, such as central tendency (mean, median, mode), variability (range, standard deviation), and distribution (skewness, kurtosis). This branch of statistics is primarily focused on describing data and does not draw conclusions beyond the data itself.

Inferential Statistics: Inferential statistics is the branch of statistics concerned with making predictions or generalizations about a larger population based on sample data. That is to say, it uses analytical techniques to draw conclusions about underlying processes or phenomena to explain the sample of data. Inferential statistics allows users to make hypotheses about the population or test their assumptions using sample data. These techniques include hypothesis testing, confidence intervals, and regression analysis, among others. Inferential statistics provides a framework for drawing meaningful conclusions and making data-driven decisions beyond the specific sample under investigation.

Design of Experiments: Design of experiments (DOE) is a statistical technique used to systematically plan, execute, and analyze experiments to understand the relationship between factors or variables and their impact on a process or outcome. DOE enables organizations to optimize processes, improve product quality, and reduce variation by identifying significant factors and their interactions. It involves carefully selecting experimental conditions, controlling variables, and collecting data to generate meaningful insights and make data-driven decisions. DOE helps organizations maximize efficiency, minimize costs, and achieve desired performance targets.

Prioritization Techniques: When there is more than one problem/issue to solve or more than one competing idea on how to solve the problem, it is valuable to both objectively decide on a path forward and collectively agree as a team that it is the "best" choice. There are multiple methods/tools to accomplish this, so use the ones that best fit your team and the issue.

Nominal Group Technique: This is a voting process whereby each team member gets a set number of votes to choose the problem to work on, or the solution to pursue. Using the N/3 rule, each teammate gets a number of votes equal to the number of options divided by three. After votes are cast by all members, you count and the leading option is moved forward.

Effort v. Impact: This technique rates each issue or solution on a two-dimensional graph of both the impact it will have and the estimated effort to resolve. After collecting ideas, a first idea is placed on the graph choosing the vertical axis of impact—"How impactful would it be on our goals to solve this problem?" or "How impactful on this problem would the proposed solution be?" Then you move the idea horizontally based on how difficult it will be to solve the problem or implement the solution. After the first idea is placed, subsequent ideas are ranked relative to the first item. Ideas should not overlap to create clear separation on the rank of ideas. The team should evaluate and potentially combine ideas in the quadrant that is "High Impact" and "Low Effort" first.

Pugh Analysis: A relative ranking of ideas that is accomplished by comparing alternatives to a one-reference idea. The team establishes criteria to rate the ideas, and often this comes from VOC interactions (above). Each idea is compared as better (+), worse (-), or same (o) to the established baseline idea. Summing up each column, the team creates separation of ideas based on the requirements of constraints. The baseline idea can come out as the "winner" or you can combine concepts into a solution.

Verification of Improvement: A crucial element of change management is building confidence in the change that is taking place.

Pilot: A pilot is a way of testing a new solution or design with a small group of users or scenarios before it is more widely implemented. Testing in a pilot gives performance feedback in a controlled environment.

Prototype: A prototype is an early model of a product or solution to test a concept or a process. It verifies effectiveness and evaluates design. The test scenario or units may not be 100 percent "production representative," but it provides indication of performance.

Simulation: A model of the process or system in operation to test independent scenarios that may be expensive, dangerous, or time-limiting. This allows the designer to change variables and get feedback to optimize the design.

Process Standardization: Process standardization is the establishment of a set of rules that constrain how a process can be executed or govern how people in an organization are to complete a given task or sequence of tasks.

Standard Operating Procedures (SOP): A document that describes operations relevant to the quality of the product or service provided. The purpose of an SOP is to document and train individuals to carry out the operations correctly and in the same manner to reduce variation.

Standard Work: Standard work refers to the agreed-upon best practices, procedures, and methods that define the safest, most effective, and efficient way to perform a specific task or process. It involves capturing the optimal sequence or work, the amount of work performed at one cycle (sometimes called the work in process, or WIP), and the target times for completion. Standard work serves as a baseline for training and continuous improvement efforts, a reference point of process and performance measurement for further optimization. It helps organizations improve productivity, reduce variation, and enhance quality.

Mistake-Proofing: A technique used to reduce or prevent error from occurring during the execution of a process, this involves designing and implementing mechanisms, devices, or controls that prevent, notify, or mitigate effects of mistakes. By eliminating or reducing the potential for errors, you improve quality and increase efficiency by avoiding rework. In some Lean deployments they use the Japanese term *poka-yoke*, which translates to "mistake-proofing."

5S: 5S is a workplace organization method that originated from the Japanese Lean manufacturing philosophy. It consists of five key principles: sort, set in order, shine, standardize, and sustain. 5S aims to create a clean, organized, and efficient work environment as the standard to begin work. This enables easier identification of abnormalities such as missing parts/tools, broken equipment, or quality issues. The principles involve removing unnecessary items (sort), arranging essential items in a logical manner (set in order), cleaning and maintaining the workspace (shine), establishing standard procedures and visual controls (standardize), and sustaining the improvements through ongoing discipline and training (sustain).

Process Control Plan: A written document used to sustain and maintain improvements and stability of operations, this outlines the process steps, tasks, or attributes that affect quality, the associated control method, and reaction plans for scenarios that are out of the set control limits.

Performance Boards: Performance Boards are both the display and structured meeting. The review is conducted at various levels within an organization to assess performance against defined metrics and KPIs. Reviews occur in tiers of the organization to serve as checkpoints, ensuring daily operations and projects align with organizational goals and information is passed on to support decision-making. These daily reviews help improve awareness, enhance accountability, and facilitate effective decision-making.

Chapter 4

SQDCM: This is an acronym that represents KPIs in the context of Lean manufacturing. It stands for safety, quality, delivery, cost, and morale. SQDCM serves as a framework for measuring and managing performance in manufacturing processes. Each component represents a critical aspect that contributes to overall operational excellence. Safety focuses on creating a safe work environment. Quality aims to meet or exceed customer expectations. Delivery emphasizes on-time delivery of products or services. Cost seeks to optimize resource utilization and minimize waste, and morale addresses employee engagement and satisfaction. SQDCM implies that you should measure and manage your processes with more than one indicator metric, thus providing a holistic view of performance to help identify areas for improvement.

Escalation: Escalation is a process of raising a problem, issue, or decision to a higher level of authority or management for resolution. It is typically used when a mistake is make, a standard procedure is not effective, or frontline efforts do not have the resource or authority to address a problem. The flow of information ensures that problems receive appropriate attention and resources from higher levels of the organization, enabling timely decision-making and resolution. Having guidance on how and when issues need to be escalated gives confidence to the teams and leadership that issues are being managed at an appropriate level.

1:3:10: This is the concept of ten-second management, whereby you should be able to identify the status of a measure or process performance in one second, see the trend of past performance leading up to the current state in three seconds, and know what actions are being taken or planned in ten seconds. This concept is more of a heuristic than a requirement. When designing visual controls or visual reporting for management of a process, the 1:3:10 guideline should be considered to enhance effectiveness of communication.

Chapter 5

Leader Standard Work: Leader Standard Work refers to the set of routine tasks, activities, and behaviors that leaders at various levels of an organization perform consistently to drive operational excellence and sustain continuous improvement efforts. It includes going to where the actual work is performed to confirm processes are executed as designed and to engage with employees. Leader Standard Work also includes reviewing performance metrics, providing feedback, and coaching problem-solving. Clear expectations for leaders' roles and responsibilities promote a culture of accountability and a foundation for sustainable improvement.

Appendix 2:
Author's Journey

WITH AN INNATE CURIOSITY, *driven to learn, and naturally competitive, I get deeply interested in new activities, hobbies, or interests. I want to get better. I want to figure it out. That natural problem-solving mindset and an affinity for math carried over into an academic pursuit in the field of engineering. I felt confident about what I wanted to do as a career. However, during an internship with a construction equipment manufacturer between my junior and senior year of college, I was sobered by the reality that "I don't actually want to be a mechanical engineer."*

After hours sitting behind a computer doing CAD and FEA analysis, the highlight of my week was visiting the production floor to speak with manufacturing about the feasibility of design changes. Then, during a senior year Design for Manufacturing course at Michigan Technological University, a phrase from Dr. Craig Friedrich resonated with me, "The best design in the world isn't worth anything if you haven't thought about how to make it."

Bingo! How to make stuff. How to make stuff consistently with good quality and reliability. That was it for me. And that domain fell within the Industrial Engineering Body of Knowledge.

So I followed this amazing girl I had met out to the East Coast and attended graduate school at Rutgers University in New Jersey and earned a degree focusing on Quality Engineering and Systems Reliability. (That girl turned out to be a pretty good bet. We have been married eighteen years now, with three kids and two dogs.)

Upon graduation I leveraged that knowledge at the US Army Armament Research, Development, and Engineering Center (ARDEC) supporting development, production, and stockpile surveillance on a portfolio of nonlethal capabilities in our military. Serendipitously, the command was piloting a new continuous improvement program at that time called Lean Six Sigma. I signed up immediately to get trained and was certified as a Green Belt, simultaneously pursuing an advanced degree in Applied Statistics.

With that skill set, I was asked to join the office deploying Lean Six Sigma and also took over as custodian of MIL-STD-1916, the DoD Preferred Method for Acceptance of Product. I got trained and certified at the Black Belt level of Six Sigma and began teaching others on process improvement and process control across the base, then the country, and eventually other countries around the world. It was here that relatively early in my career I realized two things: (1) I had a passion for learning and teaching and (2) my application niche was in process improvement.

I took this experience and awareness to a career opportunity in a new industry: medical device manufacturing. There I was able to apply the Lean and Six Sigma body of knowledge in both manufacturing and business processes. I orchestrated business processes for one of our largest commercial divisions and helped develop and deploy a Lean operating system into our global manufacturing group.

While in that role I had the opportunity to support a local nonprofit as part of the corporate giving program through skill-based volunteering. Along with a colleague we helped develop the business system starting with daily management, then introducing process improvement through problem-solving and integrating under a regular cadence of strategic planning. (I still have ties to this organization to coach and mentor.)

As the continuous improvement deployment at the med device company matured in the five plants that I had accountability for, I was recruited out of that organization to help lead the Lean transformation for a company in another industry, electric and natural gas utilities. I followed a similar story of engaging leaders, learning the business, and teaching them continuous improvement principles and tools.

We restructured the Lean operating system and aligned improvements through business plan deployment. I began to notice that more of my advanced toolset did not come out as often as early in my career. I saw that most of the problems encountered were solved with relatively simple tools. I also observed that organizations would be very focused on tools or on something they saw at a benchmarking visit or read in a book.

The most traction was gained in cases where we had focused efforts and aligned execution. While maturing the corporate (business process) arm of the business and integrating with the operations arm of the business, I began getting requests from my network to support other companies in their continuous improvement journey; facilitate problem-solving, deliver training workshops to develop capabilities, and lead strategic planning sessions.

I took this distilled approach into those organizations, and it resonated. What started as a side business grew to where I could not support both this effort and my corporate responsibilities. This aligned with my personal ambitions and mission to enable organizations for sustainable continuous improvement. I now had the ability to expand the impact I could have.

I am still obsessed with how stuff works, though now it is how businesses work. My path went from improving design to improving manufacturing to improving cross-functional support to improving business strategy to improving transformation. And I am still learning and refining.

Initial client engagements usually encompassed "part" of the business management system I advocate. The client would want strategy deployment or help with process improvement or implementing a daily management system. After the initial value was delivered, there was a clear need for another element of the system to either align or change or sustain.

I began to think about how I would engage with a client to get the right pieces in place, in the right order. I began to write those ideas down, and it became this book. Through the writing process and application in my own business and with clients, I arrived at the Improve LESS philosophy, implemented through the Focus and Align Framework^{TM}. It is a guide to that ideal engagement.

By leaning back on my character to study and learn and teach, I have whittled down an approach that matches what I have seen work. To do so I have had to challenge my own mental constructs and methods, which is the same thing I ask clients to do in their organization. I will continue to improve, and I have the management system and framework to do it. I sincerely hope it helps you as well.

www.ingramcontent.com/pod-product-compliance
Lightning Source LLC
Chambersburg PA
CBHW060539130626
46553CB00002B/827